Letter
OF THE Day

Fun Alphabet Activities for 3–5 Year Olds

Books by Talita Paolini

Read, Write, & Spell:
A Complete Guide for Home Education

Play & Learn with Cereal O's:
Language, Math, and Science

Letter

OF THE DAY

Fun Alphabet Activities for 3–5 Year Olds

Talita Paolini

Paolini International LLC
Livingston, Montana USA

Copyright ©2019 Talita Paolini

Artwork:
Copyright ©2019 Paolini International LLC
Illustrated by Jacob Meijer, Immanuela Meijer, Talita Paolini

All Rights Reserved. Reproduction or use of the contents in whole or in part without permission of the publisher is prohibited.

Published by Paolini International LLC
PO Box 343
Livingston MT 59047
USA

Visit us online: paolinimethod.com

Manufactured in the United States of America
First Edition

**Publisher's Cataloging-In-Publication Data
(Prepared by The Donohue Group, Inc.)**

Names: Paolini, Talita.
Title: Letter of the day : fun alphabet activities for 3-5 year olds / Talita Paolini.
Description: First edition. | Livingston, Montana USA : Paolini International LLC, [2019] | Series: --Of the day ; [bk. 1] | "Paolini Method, learning by doing"--Cover. | For parents and educators of 3-5 year olds.
Identifiers: ISBN 9780966621365
Subjects: LCSH: English language--Alphabet--Study and teaching (Preschool)--Activity programs. | Education, Preschool--Activity programs. | Creative activities and seatwork.
Classification: LCC LB1525.65 .P36 2018 | DDC 372.46/5--dc23

Cover design by Tara Mayberry: TeaberryCreative.com
Author photo by Immanuela Meijer

In memory of my mother,
Barbara Jane Loomis Hodgkinson,
who introduced me to the wonders of nature.

Table of Contents

Getting Started 10
A Word About Supplies 15

The Activities

Apple Tree 16
Ant Anatomy 18
Apple Bracelet 20
Animal Mobile 22

Blowing Bubbles 24
Bud, Bird, Bee! 26
Butterfly Bookmark 28
Banana Bread 30

C Picture 32
Cat Story 34
C Is for Crown 36
Caterpillar Toy 38

Counting Doors 40
Dandelion Necklace 42
Dress a Duck 44
Dinosaur Light 46

Eggshell Collage 48
Energy! 50
Yummy Eggs 52
Eggplant Elf 54

A Pretty Folded Fan 56
F Is for Flag 58

A Fishy Picture	60
Flower Brooch	62
A Bunch of Grapes	64
Plan a Garden	66
A Small Gift	68
G Is for Glass	70
Hand Print Picture	72
Heart Chain	74
Hop! Hop!	76
H Is for House	78
Insect Poster	80
How Many Inches?	82
Iggy Iguana	84
Colorful I's	86
Jam Swirl	88
Jeans and Jackets	90
A Pen Jar	92
Jet Game	94
Kite on the Wall	96
Fun with Ketchup	98
A Book of Keys	100
Popcorn Kitty	102
Lemonade	104
Watercolor Leaves	106
Miss Ladybug	108
Lettuce Wraps	110
Mustard Squirt	112
Treasure Map	114
Mushroom Mobile	116
Felt Mitten	118

N Is for Neck	120
Necklace	122
Nutshell Prints	124
Noodle Nests	126
Octopus Picture	128
Olive Appetizers	130
Octopus Doll	132
Octagon Prints	134
Popcorn Necklace	136
Peg the Porcupine	138
Polish a Penny	140
Placemat	142
Quilt	144
Quart	146
Big Q, Little q Wall Hanging	148
Question Box	150
Rock People	152
Radish Sprouts	154
Rabbit Picture	156
Rice & Raisin Pudding	158
Salt Paperweight	160
Snowman Notecard	162
Soap Bubbles	164
Spoon Sculptures	166
Walnut Shell Turtles	168
Tea Party	170
Tent	172
Tree	174
Umbrella Watercolor	176
Under and Up!	178

Rainy Day Umbrellas ... 180
U Is for Underwear ... 182

Volcano ... 184
Vanilla Milkshake ... 186
Vegetable Salad ... 188
Valentine ... 190

W Is for Wood ... 192
Walnut Balls ... 194
W Is for Water ... 196
Wood Wall Hanging ... 198

X Necklace ... 200
X Card ... 202
X Bookmark ... 204
X Sews a Button ... 206

Yellow Book ... 208
Yarn Collage ... 210
Yummy Food ... 212
Y Is for Yes! ... 214

Z Sewing Card ... 216
Sleepy zzz Book ... 218
Z Prints ... 220
Zoo Animals ... 222

Acknowledgments ... 224

Getting Started

Welcome to this fun collection of activities that help your child learn the alphabet letters. I remember doing many of these projects with my own children, creating artwork that hung by the kitchen table to be admired and referred to at mealtime. To this day they have fond memories of mixing, painting, and gluing, exploring the world using common household items.

Each letter stars in four activities that help your child remember its sound and shape. Throughout the lessons, focus on teaching the letter sounds (page 11) instead of their names. This will give him the building blocks he will use to begin reading. And say the Verbal Cues (page 13) to help him learn to trace and write the letter shapes correctly.

Some projects guide him to explore his environment and become more aware of his surroundings. He learns to focus on an object or task, ask questions about it, and then find ways to test possible answers. With your help, he also learns how to search out more information on topics of interest. Whether he remembers exact terms or results is not important, rather it's the process of discovery that opens the door to future learning.

This book includes 104 lessons, enough to last a year if you do two per week. Continue his learning adventure with my book, *Read, Write, & Spell,* which shows you how to teach language through grade three.

Tips for Doing the Activities

Let your child's interest guide the pace of the lessons. If he is enthusiastic about an activity, let him work at it as he desires. If, on the other hand, he finds a project tedious, put it away. Keep an attitude of playful exploration as you introduce the letters and he will eagerly look forward to these mini "game" sessions.

Modify the projects to your child's level of development. If he is not yet writing, have him trace the letter shapes with his fingers instead of printing them.

Bring the featured letters to his attention in different contexts throughout the day. And be patient with his progress. Young children's brains work hard to make sense of the information they receive. It is perfectly normal for them to require the introduction of a new concept multiple times before it "sticks."

A Word About Letter Sounds

Each letter has a *name* <u>and</u> one or more *sounds.* The letter *b,* for example, has the name *bee,* but its *sound* is short and explosive without any following vowel tone. (Listen to the letter sounds on our website: www.paolini.net/educators/downloadable-content/) Teach your child the names of the letters, *Aee, Bee, Cee,* etc., but emphasize the phonetic *sounds* of the letters and soon he will be able to decipher words.

Each vowel *(a, e, i, o, u)* represents two or more sounds. Notice the *a* in *cat, cake,* and *father.* To simplify, begin by teaching your child the *short* sound of each vowel, as demonstrated by these words: *cat, hen, sit, hop, hut.* This will give him the tools to begin reading simple words and sentences.

When you say the consonants (all the letters that are not the vowels—*a, e, i, o, u),* try to say just the *sound* of the letter. In our *b* example, say the word *bat.* Now say the *b* sound without the *at* that follows. The letters *b, c, d, g, j, k, p,* and *t* have short, explosive sounds. Try isolating their sounds in these words: *bat, cat, dig, gun, jam, kitten, pin,* and *top.* The sound for letter *h* is also short, but it is quietly exhaled, as in *hat.* Another short sound is *y.* Say it as in *yarn.*

The sounds for *f, l, m, n, r, s, v, w,* and *z* are held longer. Say them as the first sound in the words *fox, lamp, mop, nut, run, sit, vase, window,* and *zebra.* The letter *q* is always followed by *u* and is said *kw,* as in *quiet.* The letter *x* combines two sounds and is said *ks* as in *fox.*

How to Hold a Pencil
Pinch the pencil with the thumb and first finger just above the line where the paint meets the sharpened wood tip. Let the pencil rest on the first joint of the middle finger, as shown below. This is called the three-fingered grip. Left-handers use a similar position but should grip the pencil a bit higher, so they can see over and around their hand.

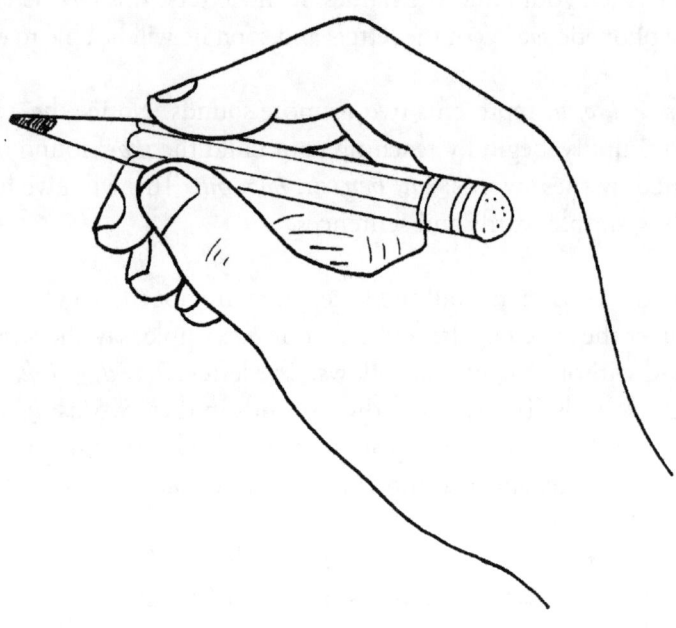

abcdefghijklmn
opqrstuvwxyz

Verbal Cues for Writing the Letters:

Use these verbal cues when demonstrating how to write the letters. Take special note of the *a* and *g,* which differ noticeably from the font used below.

a—up and around, up, down
b—down, up and around
c—up and around
d—up and around, up, down
e—across, up and around
f—curve, straight down, across
g—up and around, up, down and curve
h—down, up, over and down
i—down, dot
j—down, curve, dot
k—down, slant, slant
l—down
m—down, up and over, down, up and over, down
n—down, up and over, down
o—up and around
p—down, up and around
q—up and around, up, down
r—down, up and over
s—up and curve and curve again
t—down and across
u—down, curve, up, down
v—slant down, slant up
w—slant down, slant up, slant down, slant up
x—slant, slant
y—slant, big slant
z—across, slant, across

Enrich the Learning Experience

Letters are everywhere. Understanding them is like having a key that unlocks a mysterious code, one that eventually leads to reading. Once your child begins learning their sounds, shapes, and names, use every opportunity to bring them to her attention.

Encourage her to find letters on newspapers, magazines, and books in your home, and to point them out on billboards and signs. Make a game of looking for familiar ones on boxes of food or other supplies when shopping.

Provide her with a variety of writing tools: crayons, markers, pencils, chalk, paint brushes, etc. and cheer on her efforts. Have her scratch letters into mud or sand with a stick or trace them with her fingers in a pie plate filled with flour or cornmeal.

In addition, read aloud to your child daily. Make a habit of coming together at a certain time, perhaps as part of your evening routine. Set aside any discord and cuddle up with a favorite book. It is normal for young children to want a certain story read over and over; in fact, studies have shown that this repetition is helpful for learning. As the same material is reviewed, neural pathways are strengthened. Certainly grab a new book now and then, but understand the need to revisit "old friends" to help your child grow and learn.

I treasure the time I spent doing these activities with my children. Occasionally a lesson failed to capture their interest and was quickly put away. But I remember other events as well: the day a project expanded into a full body painting session, the exploration of plants that developed into a life-long love of botany for my daughter, and the research of dinosaurs that sparked my son's fascination with dragons and led to his writing the Inheritance Cycle.

Who knows what adventures await as you explore the world with your child? I wish you well on your journey!

Talita Paolini

A Word about Supplies

The items called for in this book are commonly available. Below are a few that require additional comment.

Lead Pencils

While a regular No. 2 lead pencil is fine to use with these lessons, younger children may be more comfortable working with a larger diameter one. If you can, provide a softer-lead pencil that produces a thick line with minimal pressure.

Colored Pencils

Writing letters with colored pencils is more enjoyable than working with plain gray. If possible, purchase a few high-quality, soft-core colored pencils (such as Prismacolor) for use with these lessons. Your child will find them easier to use than cheap ones (with harder lead) sold in discount stores because they lay down a thick line of color with little pressure. Find them labeled as "art pencils" online or in art and stationery stores.

Pictures

Many activities call for pictures, both to look at and to cut out for projects. You can collect these from a variety of places: the internet, library books, magazines, and catalogs. The internet is a great resource for finding obscure images, such as what a walnut looks like when growing on a tree.

Scissors

Choose a pair that are child safe with blunt tips. Test them to make sure they cut cleanly and easily. If your child is left handed, provide left-handed scissors. Insist that he be seated when cutting and that he pay attention to the task. Teach him how to use the scissors correctly and how to hold the paper with his other hand. Supervise cutting activities closely. If he has not used scissors before, begin by letting him snip paper to build strength in his hand muscles, refine motor skills, and improve hand-eye coordination. When he has practiced this awhile, have him cut along straight lines. Finally, give him curved lines and circles to cut.

༈ A ༈

Apple Tree

Use this idea to make other fruit or nut trees (pear, peach, mango, lemon, grapefruit, banana, coconut, walnut, or hazelnut), while emphasizing the first letter of each one.

☞ **What You Need:**

An apple; white, red, green, and yellow construction paper; glue; colored markers; scissors; pencil

✂ **To Prepare:**

1. Use green and brown markers to draw a tree on a large sheet of white construction paper. This is the Apple Tree paper.

2. With pencil, draw apple shapes onto red, green, and yellow construction paper.

☆ **Activity:**

1. Show your child the apple. Encourage him to look at it closely and to smell and feel it. Discuss his observations. Explain that an apple grows on a tree. Point out the stem that attached it to the tree and the blossom end, the remains of the flower.

2. Slice the apple. Invite him to smell and taste it and then tell you what he is experiencing.

3. Now give him the prepared Apple Tree paper. Tell him that the word for apple begins with the letter *a*. (Be sure to say the letter's sound. See A Word About Letter Sounds, page 11.) With black marker, write a large *a* on the right lower corner of the paper.

4. Ask him to trace over the large *a* with a pencil, then write the letter on the red, green, and yellow apples outlined earlier and cut them out.

5. Invite him to glue the *a* apples on the Apple Tree. Have him say the *a* sound each time he attaches one.

Variation:

Cut out a large construction paper tree and attach it to a bulletin board, on a piece of poster board, or directly on a wall. Follow the steps above, taping (instead of gluing) on the apples.

❦ A ❦

ANT ANATOMY

Explore the world of insects with this simple lesson. Try adapting it for other species such as butterflies, beetles, earwigs, millipedes, or flies.

☞ **What You Need:**
An ant, sheet of paper, pencil

☆ **Activity:**
1. Find an ant with your child. If possible, watch a group of ants outdoors. Observe how they work together, coordinating their food collection. Notice how they are able to carry bits of stuff larger than they are. See if you can follow them back to their home.

2. Ask your child to look at one ant closely and tell you what parts she sees.

3. Discuss how the different parts are important to the insect.

4. Invite her to draw an ant on a sheet of paper. Write *ant* at the top of the paper and point out the *a*. Demonstrate how to write the letter while saying its verbal cue (up and around, up, down). Ask her to add more *a*'s of her own along the bottom of the paper, saying its sound each time. Help her label the parts of the insect, drawing attention to *abdomen* and *antenna*, which also begin with the letter *a*.

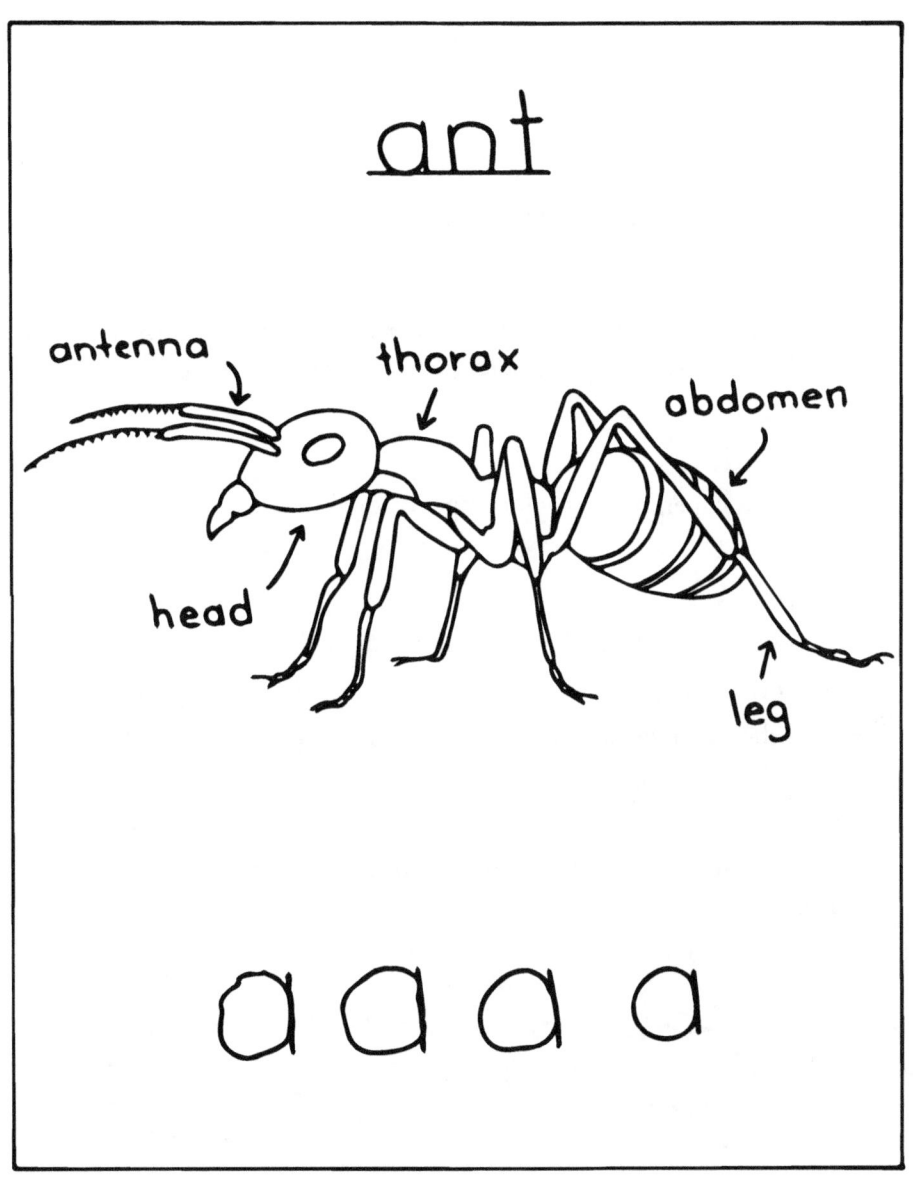

◈ A ◈

Apple Bracelet

This simple craft project will help your child remember the letter a. *When people comment on the colorful bracelet, he can respond that is it his apple bracelet and that* a *is for* apple!

☞ **What You Need:**
   Construction paper, scissors, glue, tape, colored marker

☆ **Activity:**

1. With your child, cut small apple shapes from colorful construction paper.

2. Write *a* on one of the apples. Say it's sound. Explain that *a* is the first letter of the word *apple*. Invite him to write lots of *a's* on the other apples.

3. Demonstrate, then have him overlap the side edges of the apple shapes and secure them with dots of glue. When the chain is long enough so he can comfortably slip his hand through when it is formed into a bracelet, lay it flat to dry.

4. Complete the bracelet by taping the ends together.

Apple Bracelet • 21

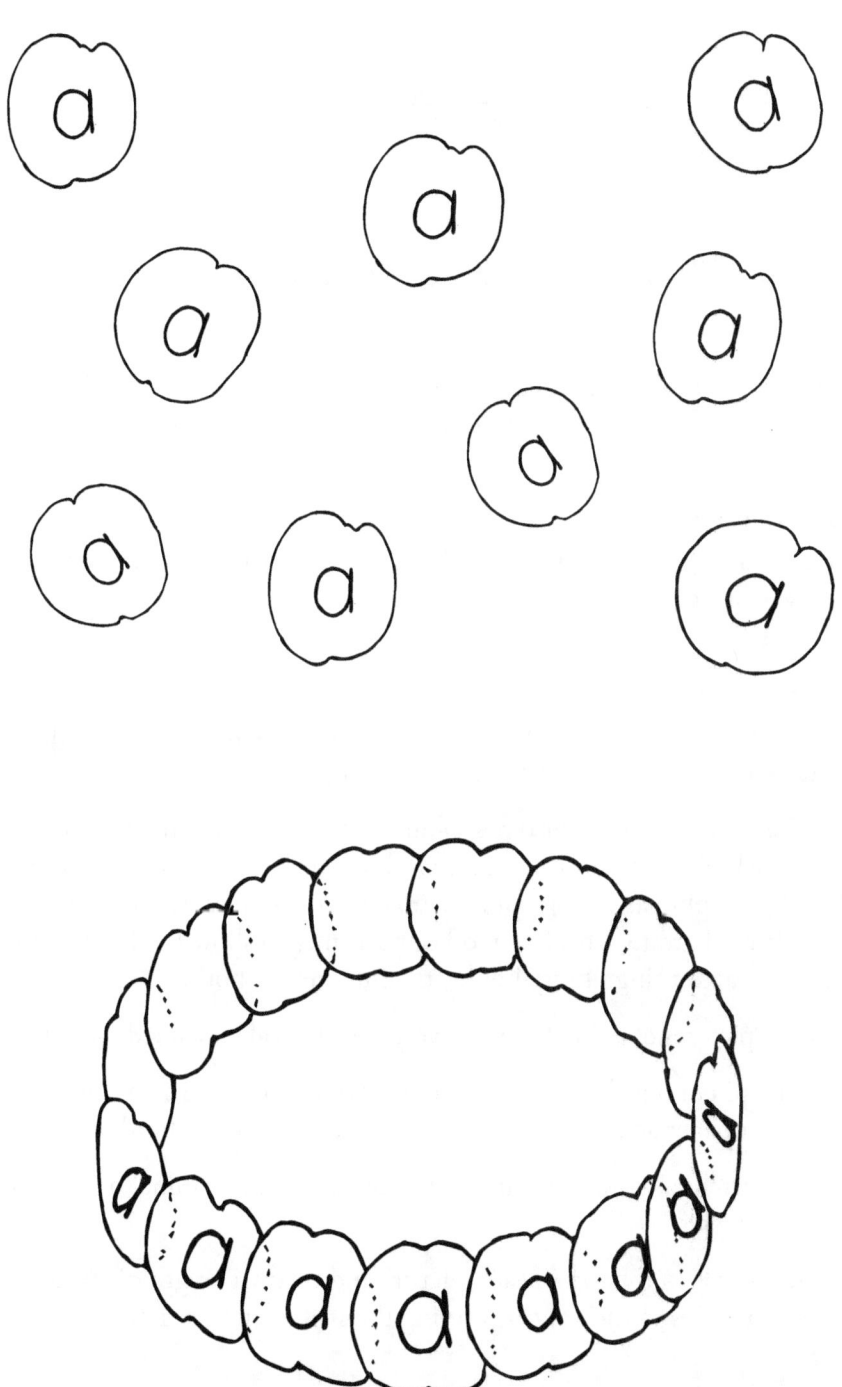

A

Animal Mobile

Use this project to launch a discussion about animals. Not only will your child learn the letter a, *she will learn about the diversity of creatures in the animal kingdom.*

☞ **What You Need:**

Hanger, yarn or string, paper, pencil, construction paper, pictures of animals, glue, scissors, colored marker

☆ **Activity:**

1. Tell your child that *a* is the first letter in the word *animal.* Write the letter and have her practice printing it and saying its sound.

2. Ask her to name different types of animals. Be sure she includes some from each of these groups: mammals, birds, fish, reptiles (snakes and lizards), amphibians (frogs and salamanders), and insects. Discuss what defines each group. This is a good opportunity to show her how to do basic research using library books, the internet, or both.

3. Collect pictures of animals, or—if you are artistically inclined—draw them.

4. Ask her to cut out five or six of her favorites, then glue them onto construction paper and cut around them, leaving a colorful border.

5. As she watches, write the name of the corresponding animal on the back of each image.

6. Punch a hole in the top of each picture and tie on a length of string. Then tie the pictures to the hanger, varying the string lengths, as shown.

7. To complete the project, fold a 4-inch by 5½-inch sheet of paper in half lengthwise. Cut a hole in the top and write "animals" on he front. Slip it over the top of the hanger.

~ B ~

Blowing Bubbles

Mix up a batch of bubble solution, put on some lively music, then invite your child to make and catch as many bubbles as he can!

☞ **What You Need:**
Bubble solution; pipe cleaners, potato masher, slotted spoon, or other items to use as wands; paper; marker

✄ **To Prepare:**
Make the bubble solution by mixing together the following until well dissolved:

1 cup warm water
2 tablespoons glycerin
4 tablespoons dishwashing liquid

☆ **Activity:**
1. With a marker, draw a large *b* on a sheet of paper. Demonstrate, then invite your child to trace it with his fingers and say its sound. Tell him that *b* is for bubbles and that he is are going to make some.

2. Set out one or more items that he will use for wands. If using pipe cleaners, show him how to make a loop at the top.

3. Again point out the letter *b* and encourage him to repeat the phrase "*b* is for bubbles!" Then invite him to make lots of them.

B

Bud, Bird, Bee!

Although this project focuses attention on b, *the idea can be used for any letter. When displayed on a wall or bulletin board, the finished piece is a daily reminder of the letter's sound and shape.*

What You Need:
Construction paper, colored markers, scissors, glue

Activity:
1. Place the supplies on a table and invite your child to sit with you. Explain that she is going to make a *b* picture. Write the letter *b* on the bottom corner of a sheet of construction paper. Say the *b* sound and trace the letter with your finger in the pattern you would write it. Encourage her to repeat your actions several times.

2. Together, draw and cut out simple *bud, bird, bee, bug,* and *butterfly* shapes from colored construction paper. Emphasize the *b* sound of each item as you say its name.

3. Invite her to arrange the images artfully on the page—trying different designs until she finds one she likes—then glue the pieces in place. Let dry.

4. Attach the picture to a wall or bulletin board and refer to it daily.

Bud, Bird, Bee! • 27

B

Butterfly Bookmark

Making bookmarks focuses your child's attention on books and reading. Encourage him to make a set for his own use and extras for friends. When giving a book as a gift, personalize it with one of these colorful Butterfly Bookmarks.

☞ What You Need:

Cardstock, construction paper or tissue paper, clear contact paper, scissors, ruler, glue

✂ To Prepare:

1. Cut out several $1^1/_2$-inch by 8-inch pieces of cardstock. These will become the bookmarks.

2. Cut an equal number of $8^1/_4$-by 2-inch pieces of clear contact paper. Do not remove the backing.

☆ Activity:

1. Explain to your child that today he is doing a project with the letter *b*. Say that the words *book, bookmark,* and *butterfly* all start with *b*. Invite him to say, "*b* book, *b* bookmark, *b* butterfly." Write a letter *b* at the top of the bookmark. Encourage him to say the letter's sound and trace it several times with his fingers or a pencil.

2. Show him how to cut out and form butterflies with scraps of colorful construction or tissue paper, arrange them on the blank bookmark, and then tack them in place with thin smudges of glue.

3. Now have him remove the backing from a piece of precut clear contact paper and hand it to you. Center it over the bookmark so a bit extends on all four sides, then gently press it down.

4. Snip a small square from each corner of the contact paper, as shown. Fold the edges and press.

B

Banana Bread

Children love to measure and stir together ingredients that somehow, almost magically, transform themselves into something altogether new . . . and tasty!

☞ **What You Need:**
Banana bread ingredients (see recipe), oven, wooden skewer

☆ **Activity:**
1. Introduce the activity by asking your child what ingredients she thinks are in banana bread. Then set out and discuss the ingredients in a recipe of your choice or the one given.

2. Measure the 2 cups of flour into a medium-sized bowl and ask her to trace lots of *b*'s in it with her fingers while saying its sound. Then say, "*b* is for banana, *b* is for bread." Explain that this flour is the first ingredient in the bread she will make. Then follow the recipe, letting her do as much as possible.

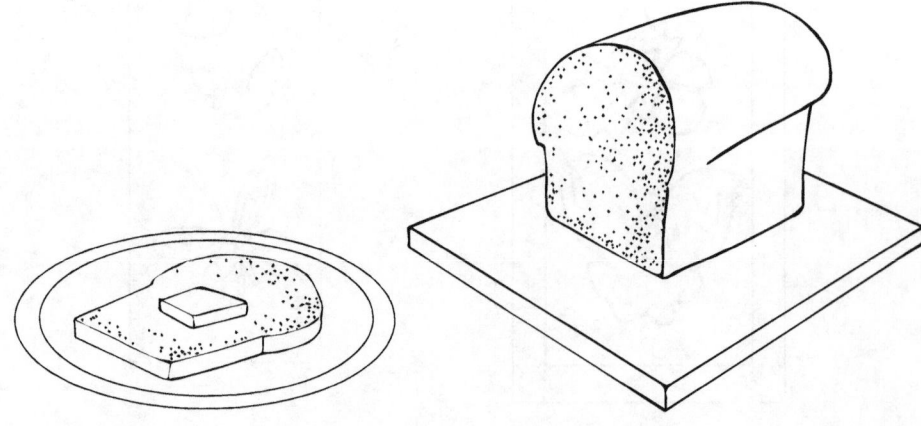

Banana Bread

Preheat the oven to 350 degrees. Show your child how to rub shortening or oil all over the inside of a 9 x 5 inch loaf pan. Sprinkle flour over the grease and tap to coat all sides. Invert the pan and tap again to remove the excess.

Step 1
In a medium bowl stir together:
2 cups flour
$3/4$ cup sugar
$1/2$ teaspoon salt
$1/2$ teaspoon baking soda

Step 2
In a large bowl mix:
$1 3/4$ cups mashed ripe banana
$1/4$ cup orange juice
2 large or 3 medium eggs, lightly beaten
6 tablespoons butter, melted and cooled
1 teaspoon vanilla extract

Step 3
Stir the dry ingredients into the bowl of wet ingredients.

Step 4 (Optional)
Stir in:
1 cup walnuts or pecans, toasted and chopped
and/or
1 cup raisins or chopped dried fruit

Step 5
Spoon the batter into the prepared loaf pan and bake in the center of the oven at 350 degrees for approximately an hour. When the top is golden brown, poke a wooden skewer into the loaf; it will come out clean when the bread is done. Let cool before slicing. Now enjoy a piece with your child and invite her to share it with others!

✢ C ✢

C Picture

Glue the corn kernels starting from the top of the c *to reinforce how the letter's shape is written.*

☞ What You Need:
Bowl of dry field corn or unpopped popcorn, construction paper, colored marker, glue, scissors

✂ To Prepare:
Choose a sheet of construction paper that contrasts with the corn and cut in half. With marker, draw a large letter *c* on the paper.

☆ Activity:
1. Introduce the project by telling your child that *c* is the first letter in the world *corn*. Have him say *c, corn* with you several times.

2. Show him the prepared paper. Say, "This is *c*." Ask him to repeat the sound. Demonstrate, then have him trace the letter with his fingers three times.

3. Bring out the bowl of corn. Show him how to place a dab of glue on the line and press in one or more kernels. Invite him to complete the project on his own. Let the picture dry flat.

4. Hang the finished piece on a wall or bulletin board. Encourage him to trace the *c* shape and say its sound often.

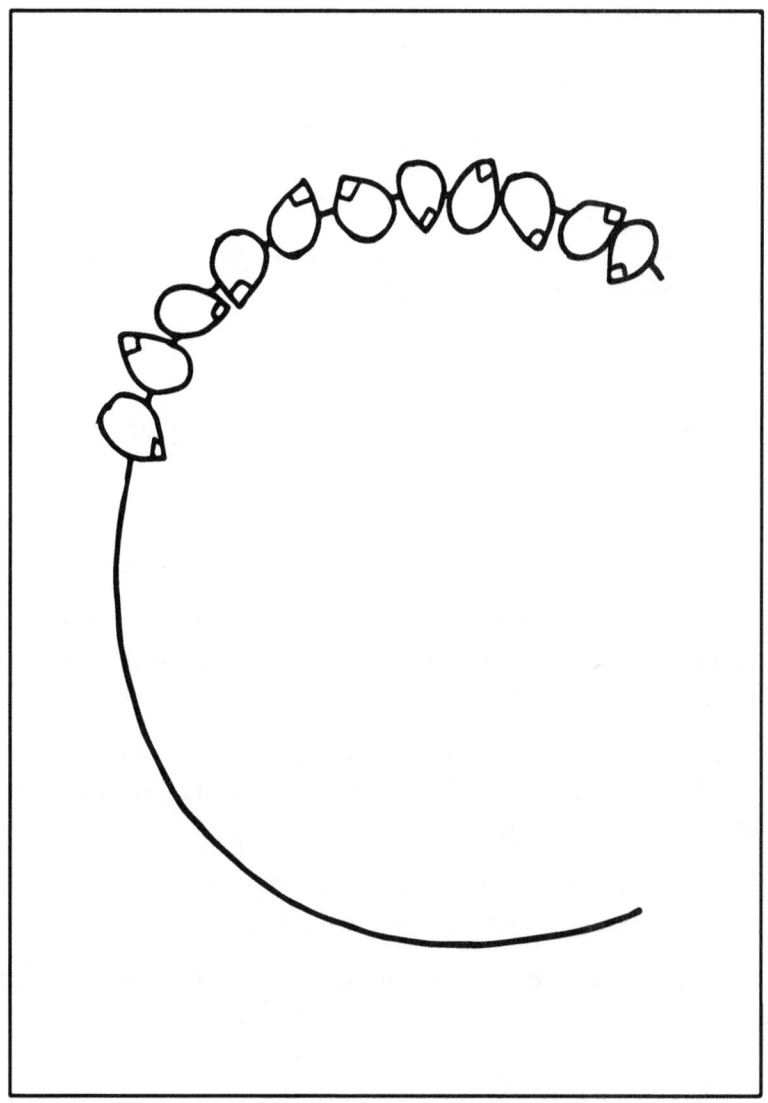

~ C ~

Cat Story

What adventure has kitty been having? As you jot down your child's tale, she sees that her speech can be recorded with written words.

☞ **What You Need:**
   Cat pictures, construction paper, lined paper, scissors, glue

☆ **Activity:**

1. Invite your child to look at several cat pictures and cut out her favorite.

2. Ask her to give the cat a name, then think about what it might be doing and invent a short story about it. Alternately, she could simply describe the kitty.

3. Now tell her that *c* is the first letter in *cat*. Have her glue the cat picture at the top of a sheet of construction paper. Demonstrate, then have her write lots of *c*'s around the image.

4. Ask her to recount her story and watch as you write it on lined paper. When finished, read back what you have written.

5. Glue the story onto the construction paper, under the cat. Invite her to share her project with friends so they can read it too.

Pumpkin

Pumpkin is a funny cat. He likes to hide my socks. One day I found a whole pile of them under the sofa. Now I keep my socks in a drawer.

~ C ~

C Is for Crown

In addition to an art activity, this lesson includes discussion about caring for others.

☞ **What You Need:**
Construction paper, ruler, scissors, glue, stapler or tape, crayons

☆ **Activity:**
1. Ask your child to choose a color of construction paper. From it, cut a 4-inch-wide strip to fit around his head, with a little extra for overlap. Glue together several strips if you need extra length.

2. Write the letter *c* in the center of the strip. Say, "*c* is for *crown.*" Have him trace the letter with his fingers and repeat the sound several times.

3. Explain that he will make a "*c* crown" for himself. Cut the top edge of the paper into a fanciful pattern, then invite him to write *c*'s all over the strip. Have him decorate the crown with crayons and glued-on bits of colored paper.

4. Wrap the strip around his head. Glue, staple, or tape the overlapping ends together.

5. Now let your little prince (or princess) find a blanket, scarf, or piece of fabric for a cape. Explain that *c* also means caring. As the royal bearer of the *c* crown, he should think of something that shows kindness and caring for someone . . . then do it!

C Is for Crown • 37

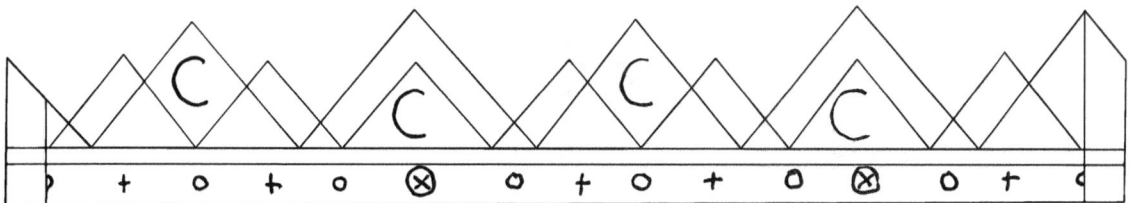

～ C ～

CATERPILLAR TOY

Once your child makes this toy, she will always remember the letter c.

☞ What You Need:
Empty cardboard egg carton, pipe cleaners, scissors, colored markers, yarn or string

✂ To Prepare:
Cut out the individual egg carton cups.

☆ Activity:
1. Introduce the lesson by telling your child about the life cycle of butterflies. Explain that butterflies lay eggs that in turn hatch into caterpillars. The caterpillars eat and grow bigger. One day each one forms a chrysalis—a special hiding place—where it stays for many days. When it comes out, it has changed into a butterfly!

2. Tell her that today she is going to make a pretend caterpillar out of an empty egg carton. Say that the word *caterpillar* begins with the letter *c*. Encourage her to say the *c* sound several times.

3. Take one egg carton cup and write *c* on it. Invite her to use assorted colored markers to write a *c* on every cup.

4. Punch holes in the sides of the cups, then help her link them with short pieces of pipe cleaners pushed through the holes. Fold the ends over inside the cups to secure.

5. Attach two pipe cleaner antennae to the front cup. Draw on two eyes and a smile. Poke a hole in the top of the head, then thread through a piece of yarn or string and knot the ends to make a pull string.

6. Now look at the finished caterpillar and give your child a hug. Compliment her on the *c*'s that she wrote. Send her off to give her new caterpillar friend a tour of your home and see if she can find any more things that start with the letter *c*.

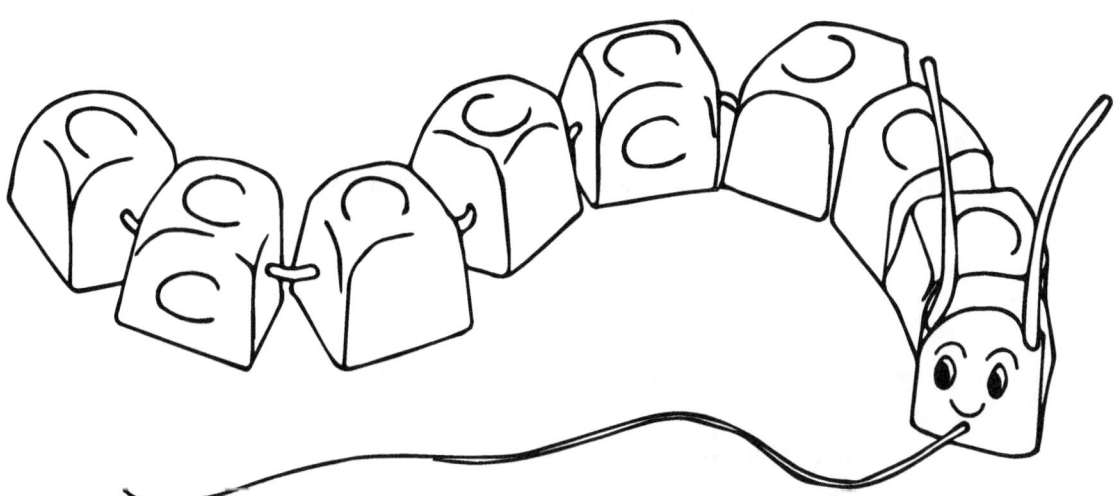

D

Counting Doors

In addition to becoming familiar with the letter d, *this activity helps your child become more aware of his environment while associating numbers with things. How many doors can he find?*

What You Need:
Construction or plain paper, scissors, colored marker, tape

To Prepare:
Cut several sheets of paper into quarters.

Activity:

1. Ask your child, "Do you know what a door is?" When he says yes, tell him to count the doors in your home. If he is very young, help him touch and count each one.

2. Together, count out the same number of prepared sheets of paper as you have doors. Write numbers (in order and beginning with 1) at the tops of the sheets.

3. Say, "*d* is for *door*" and show him how to write the letter *d*. Invite him to write a *d* beneath each number, saying its name each time.

4. Now send him off to tape one tag on each door!

Note: If you don't want tape on your doors, glue or tape yarn to the back of the cards and have him hang them on the doorknobs.

Counting Doors • 41

Variation 1:
Write the name of different doors (kitchen door, basement door, Jasmine's bedroom door, front door, etc.) on cards, then have your child match them to their correct spots.

Variation 2:
Challenge him to find and name other kinds of doors, such as cupboard, refrigerator, oven, kitchen cabinet, bathroom cabinet, cat or dog, sliding, screen, and car doors.

D

Dandelion Necklace

Turn those pesky weeds into a lesson on the letter d. *The bright, sunny yellow flowers make a charming, if fleeting, necklace.*

☞ **What You Need:**
Dandelion flowers, paper, colored pencils, crayons or markers

☆ **Activity:**

1. Ask your child if she can think of a flower that begins with the letter *d.* Tell her that daisies, daylilies, and dandelions all begin with *d.* Have her say *d, dandelion* and practice writing the letter.

2. Go outside and have her pick a dandelion. Look at it together and discuss what you observe. Are there any little insects on the flower?

3. Together, search for and pick a handful of long-stemmed dandelions. Demonstrate how to make a slit in the stem with a fingernail and push through another stem. Link the flowers, as shown, to make a necklace.

4. Suggest she look for the perfect dandelion while she wears her necklace. When she finds it, have her bring it indoors, place it in a glass of water, and then draw it, adding one or more *d*'s on the page. Now display the page where the whole family can admire it!

Note: Explain that because dandelions grow in so many places, they are considered weeds. Therefore, she can pick as many as she likes and there will always be more. In contrast, she should not pick other wildflowers without asking permission. Some plants are rare. If she picks their flowers, they can't make seeds to reproduce.

❧ D ❧

DRESS A DUCK

Once upon a time there was a duck with no feathers, oh my! Enlist your child's help in dressing the bird with colorful plumage.

☞ **What You Need:**
Construction paper, colored marker, glue, feather-shaped bits of paper or craft feathers (real feathers sold in craft stores)

☆ **Activity:**
1. With your child watching, draw a simple outline of a duck on a sheet of construction paper. Write the word *duck* at the top of the page. Point out the letter *d* and say its sound. Say *d, duck* with him several times.

2. Explain that this duck has no feathers, but that he is going to help it get dressed. Demonstrate how to glue on one real or paper feather, then invite him to continue gluing feathers until he is satisfied with the picture. Let the project dry before displaying it on a wall or bulletin board.

Dress a Duck • 45

❦ D ❧

Dinosaur Light

After seeing the dinosaur glow in a darkened room, ask your child if she can find a name for it, one that starts with d, *such as Danica, David, Donna, Danny, Dawn, Devon, Daisy, Dax, Drake, or Dustin.*

☞ **What You Need:**
Foil, scissors, ruler, thin paper (such as tracing or tissue paper), pencil, toothpick, carpet, votive candle (flame or electric), match

☆ **Activity:**

1. Explain that *d* is for dinosaur. Have your child say *d, dinosaur* several times.

2. Cut two 13- by 7-inch rectangles, one from foil and one from the thin paper.

3. On the thin paper, draw a dinosaur pattern—along with a *d*—making sure to leave a bit of space on all sides.

4. Set the foil on the carpet and lay the pattern over it. Show your child how to press down and hold the project securely with one hand while pricking holes with a toothpick along the dinosaur outline and the *d* with the other. Supervise closely during this process.

5. Roll the foil into a cylinder, folding over the ends to secure. Carefully light the candle. Lower the cylinder around it, then turn out the lights and watch the glow flicker through the holes, making the dinosaur appear out of the darkness.

Note: Be sure to supervise this activity closely if you are using a traditional candle. Extinguish the flame when you are done.

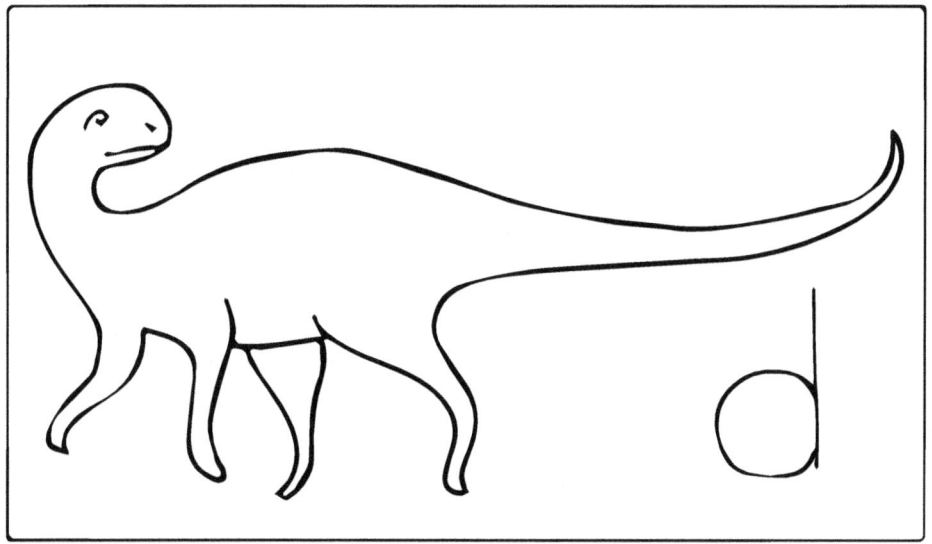

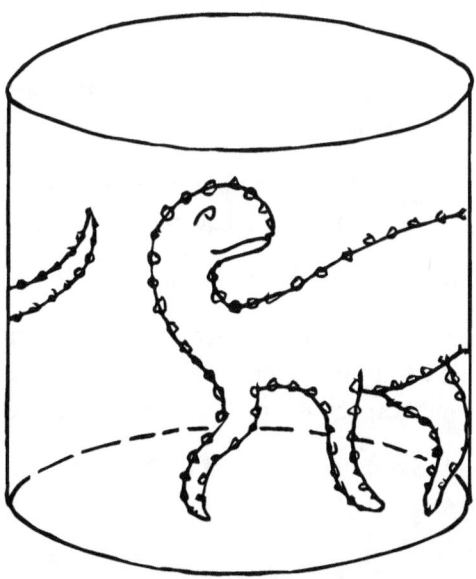

E

Eggshell Collage

Your child will love smashing up eggshells for his collage. What fun!

☞ **What You Need:**
   White eggshells, plastic bag, rolling pin or can, several small bowls, food dye, glue, waxed paper, construction paper, plain paper, marker

✂ **To Prepare:**
   Collect eggshells, removing their inner membranes. Let dry.

☆ **Activity:**
   1. With your child watching, write the letter *e* on a small piece of plain paper with marker. Together, practice saying its sound. Explain that *e* is for *egg*. Take a few moments to discuss what eggs are and where they come from. Keep the letter on the table during the activity.

   2. Place the collected eggshells in the plastic bag and have him crush them with a rolling pin or can. Shake the bag and reroll a few times.

   3. Divide the shells into several bowls and toss with food dye to color.

   4. Have him spread the bits, divided by color, onto separate sheets of waxed paper and set aside to dry overnight. The next day, pour the colored eggshells back into their respective bowls and continue the activity.

   5. Now ask him to glue the small paper with the letter *e* onto a sheet of construction paper.

6. Demonstrate how to drizzle or spread glue onto the same sheet of construction paper and sprinkle on eggshells. Invite him to complete the collage himself.

7. Let the artwork dry completely, then display.

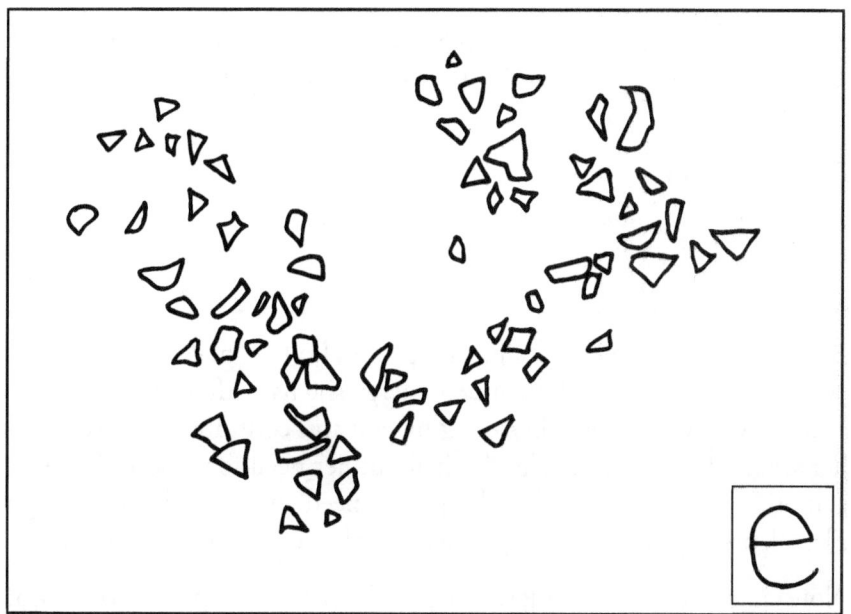

～ E ～

Energy!

This lively lesson helps your child think about what powers both herself and all the things around her. And it ends by encouraging her to use her energy to help others.

☞ What You Need:
Paper, pencil, crayon or colored pencil, yarn, scissors

☆ Activity:

1. Begin the activity by discussing energy and how it "makes things go." Tell your child to show you how much energy she has. After she has bounced around for awhile, invite her to sit by you and continue the lesson. Ask her where she gets her energy. Talk about her need for food to fuel her activities. Then mention that things also need energy to make them go. Flashlights need batteries, lights need electricity, cars need fuel, etc.

2. Now cut a circle from a quarter sheet of paper and write an *e* on it with pencil. Have her say, "*e* is for *energy*" a few times. Ask her to trace over the letter with her fingers, and then again with crayon or colored pencil.

3. Make a pendant by poking two holes in the top of the paper and looping through a length of yarn.

4. Suggest she wear her *e* pendant and show it to friends, and then demonstrate just how much energy she has by helping them with some task!

ℰ

Yummy Eggs

Here's an easy recipe that you can adjust to taste. Your child can proudly serve friends and family these lovely appetizers that he helps make.

☞ **What You Need:**
Large saucepan, water, six to twelve raw eggs, large bowl, small bowl, ice, mayonnaise, salt, pepper, fresh or dried parsley, (paprika, optional), mustard, plate, knife, fork, spoon, paper, colored pencils or markers

☆ **Activity:**
1. Have your child gently set the eggs into a pot. Cover with cold water. Bring to a boil, then turn off the heat and let sit for 12–14 minutes.

2. While the eggs are cooking, show him how to write the letter *e* or the word *egg*. Encourage him to write the letter or word several times using different colors of pencils or markers.

3. Drain the eggs and plunge them into a large bowl of ice water. Let sit for 15 minutes.

4. Together, crack and peel the eggs.

5. Carefully slice the eggs in half lengthwise. Show him how to pry out the yolks and place them in the small bowl. Set the hollow white halves on the plate.

6. Now let him smash the yolks with a fork or potato masher, along with enough mayonnaise to make a stiff paste. Add mustard, salt, pepper, and parsley to taste.

7. Demonstrate, then have him fill the whites with spoonfuls of the mixture. Garnish with a sprig of fresh parsley or a sprinkle of paprika, if desired.

8. Now have a little party with the yummy eggs, some crackers, and cups of warm tea! Cover the remaining appetizers with plastic wrap and refrigerate.

E

Eggplant Elf

This fanciful art project is a sure way to bring attention to the letter e. *Make one, make two, make an entire Eggplant Elf family!*

☞ **What You Need:**
Construction paper, scissors, glue, colored marker, eggplant (optional)

☆ **Activity:**
1. If possible, show your child a real eggplant. Together, feel it, smell it, and discuss your observations. If you don't have a real eggplant, look at a picture of one. In either case, find images showing the plant it grows on. What color are the blossoms that will become the vegetable?

2. Cut the parts (body, arms, head, decorative elements) for your Eggplant Elf from construction paper, using the illustration as a guide. Invite your child to draw on a face, then arrange the parts and glue them in place.

3. Write (or have her write) the letter *e* on the elf. Together, say, "*e* is for *eggplant* and *e* is for *elf*" several times, then display the art where she can refer to it often.

Variation:
Make a bulletin board garden with different vegetables cut from construction paper. Give each vegetable a face and write on the first letter of its name.

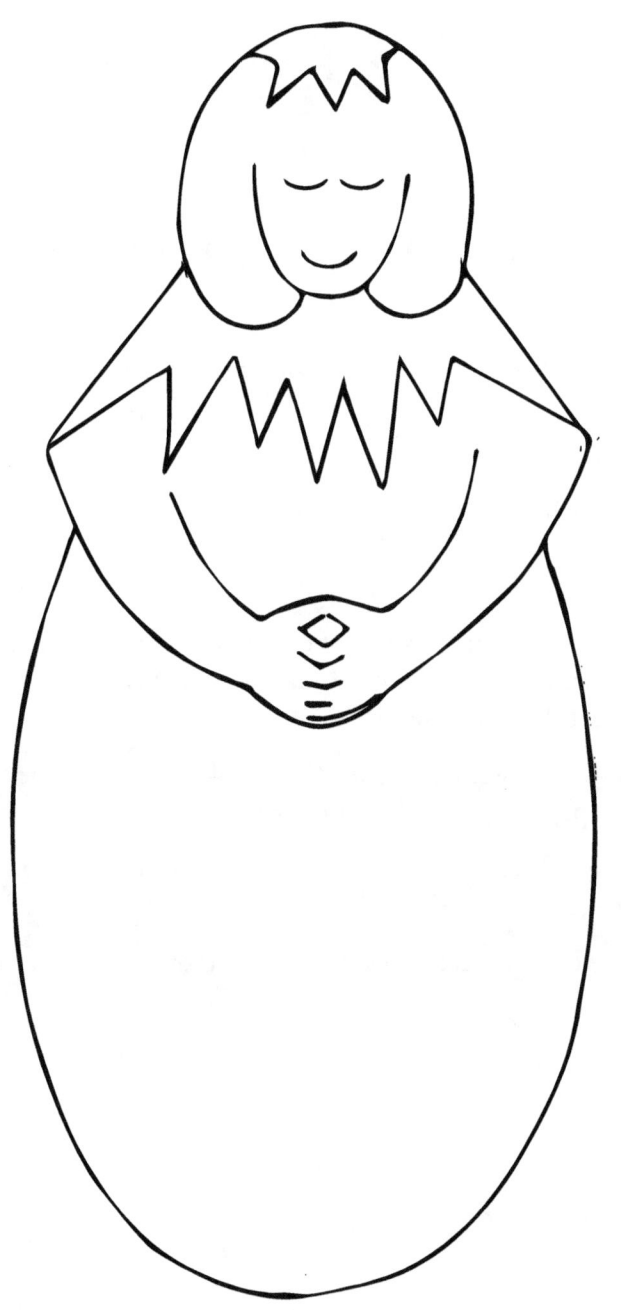

✿ F ✿

A Pretty Folded Fan

Here's a quick project that is perfect for a warm summer day.

☞ **What You Need:**
Construction paper, crayon or colored markers, stapler

☆ **Activity:**
1. Invite your child to pick a sheet of construction paper in the color of his choice. Explain that he will make a fan with it. Say, "*f* is for *fan*" and ask him to repeat the phrase several times.

2. Show him how to write the letter *f*, then ask him to write it all over both sides of the paper, using different colors of crayons or markers.

3. Fold the paper back and forth accordion style to make the fan. Staple the bottom to secure.

4. If he enjoyed the project, suggest he make another fan in a different color.

A Pretty Folded Fan • 57

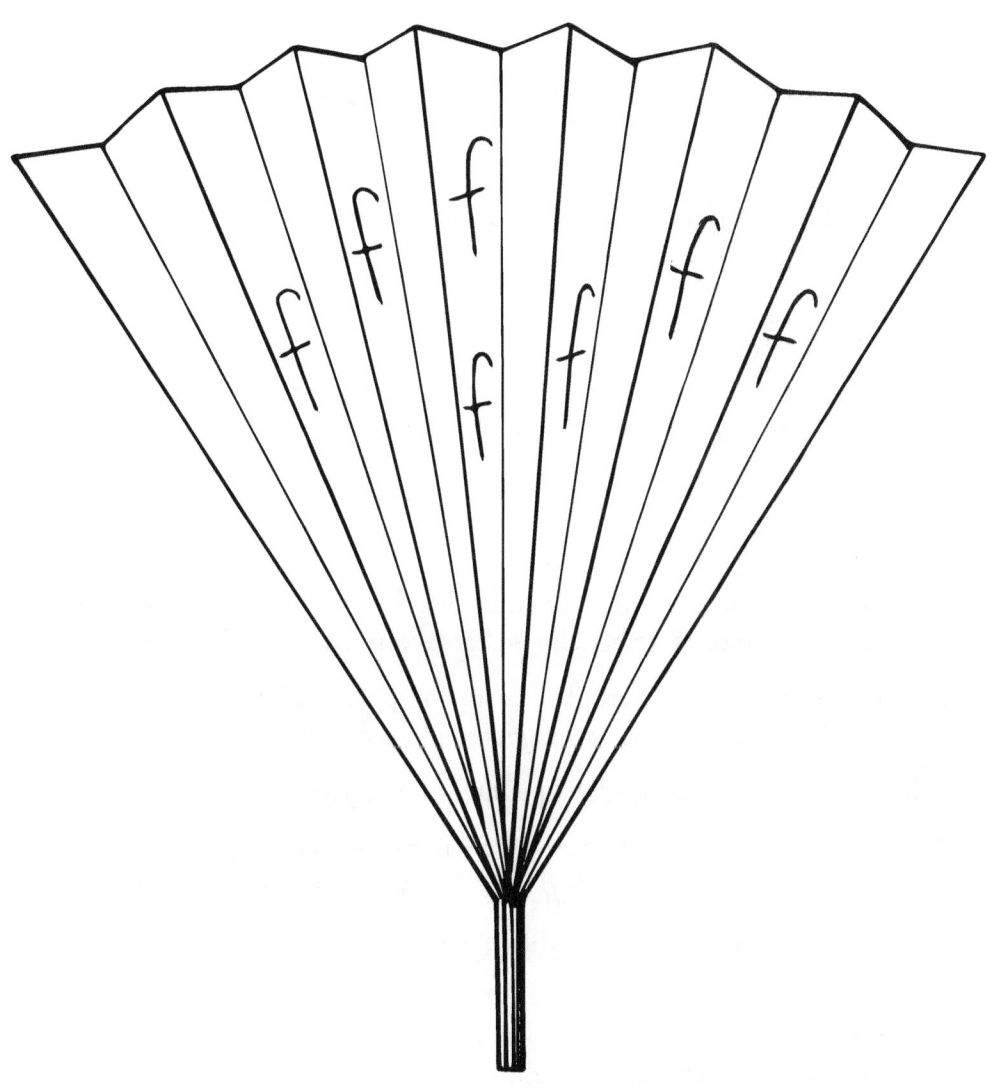

F

F Is for Flag

One of the great things about this activity is that the lesson is reinforced when your child shows her project to others.

☞ **What You Need:**
Construction paper, colored markers, scissors, glue, thin wooden dowel, pictures of things that begin with the letter *f*, such as *frog, flower, fish,* and *fork*

☆ **Activity:**
1. Look at the *f* pictures with your child. Say the name of each item, emphasizing the *f* sound. Have her choose her favorites and cut them out.

2. Write the letter *f* on a sheet of construction paper. Ask her to trace over it several times with a pencil, saying its sound each time.

3. Invite her to arrange and glue *f* pictures on the page.

4. Now have her "tell you the story" by pointing to the letter *f* and each picture in turn, saying "*f, fish; f, frog; f, flower; f, fork*" and so forth.

5. Wrap one of the short sides of the construction paper around the dowel and glue to secure. Let dry.

6. Complete the activity by playing some rousing music so she can march around the house with her *f* flag!

❧ F ☙

A Fishy Picture

Help your child explore the watery world of fish with this combination alphabet project and natural science lesson.

☞ **What You Need:**
Construction paper, pictures of fish, plain paper, thick pieces of crayon (paper removed)

☆ **Activity:**
1. Draw a fish. Point out the head, tail, fins, eyes, and mouth. Ask your child what he knows about fish. Discuss the fact that they live in salt water oceans and fresh water lakes and streams. Look at pictures of different varieties of fish and point out the similarities and differences in their sizes, shapes, and colors.

2. Now write an *f* by your fish drawing. Say, "*f* is for *fish.*" Have your child say *f, fish* several times.

3. Ask him to draw and cut out several fish shapes from construction paper. Assist as needed.

4. Demonstrate how to place the fish shapes between two pieces of plain paper and rub the side of a thick crayon firmly across the top sheet to produce an image.

5. Invite him to make more Fishy Pictures of his own, adding the letter *f* to complete the work.

A Fishy Picture

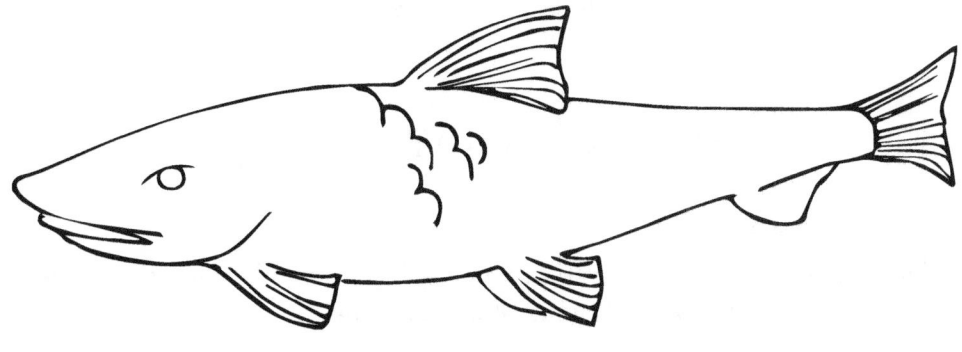

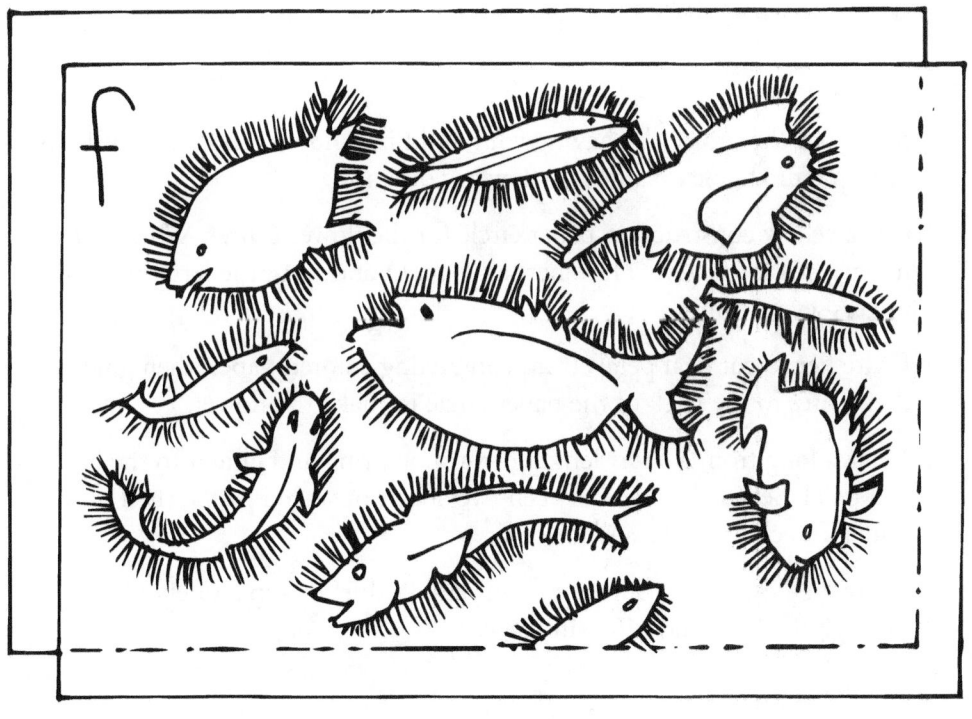

❦ F ❦

Flower Brooch

The letter f stands not only for flowers *but for* family *and* friends. *Point this out and suggest your child make Flower Brooches for her loved ones.*

☞ **What You Need:**
Construction paper, scissors, glue, colored markers, yarn or string, waxed paper, safety pin (optional)

☆ **Activity:**

1. Introduce the project by having your child find flowers indoors, outdoors, or in picture books. Name any flowers you know.

2. Cut a yellow construction paper circle for the flower center. Write an *f* on it. Say, "*f* is for *flower.*" Have her say *f, flower* and trace the letter with her fingers several times.

3. Invite her to cut oval petals from contrasting colored paper, then glue their bases to the back of the paper circle to make the flower.

4. Make a loop from a short length of yarn or string and glue it to the back of a petal. Set the brooch between two sheets of waxed paper, then press under a stack of books and let dry.

5. Hang the flower on a button of your child's shirt or slip a safety pin through the loop and pin it in place.

Flower Brooch • 63

~ G ~

A Bunch of Grapes

Dip and press a carrot end in paint to make a bunch of grapes. What fun! Your child might like to make a collection of bunches in different colors.

☞ **What You Need:**
Carrot, knife, poster paint, construction paper, colored markers, pencil, disposable styrofoam tray or pie pan, pictures of grapes, real bunch of grapes (optional)

☆ **Activity:**
1. With your child watching, write a large letter *g* in the corner of a sheet of construction paper. Be sure to say the verbal cues (page 13)—up and around, up, down, and curve—while your write. Explain that *g* is the first letter in *grapes*. Have him trace the letter with a pencil and practice saying *g, grapes*.

2. Tell him that grapes grow on vines. Some are dried to make raisins. Others are squeezed to make juice and wine. Together, look at pictures of many varieties of grapes and note that some are sweet, others tart; some are seeded, others are not; and that they come in green, blue, red, and purple. If possible, look at and taste some of the fruit.

3. Ask him what color grapes he would like to make a picture of. Pour the matching paint into a styrofoam tray or pie pan.

4. Cut the carrot in half crosswise. Demonstrate how to dip the carrot end into the paint and press it onto the paper to make grape shapes. Invite him to make a big bunch of grapes. Draw on a brown stem at the top with marker.

5. Encourage him to make as many grape pictures as he wants, writing a *g* on each page. Hang the collection beneath a green vine made of thick yarn or strips of construction paper, if desired.

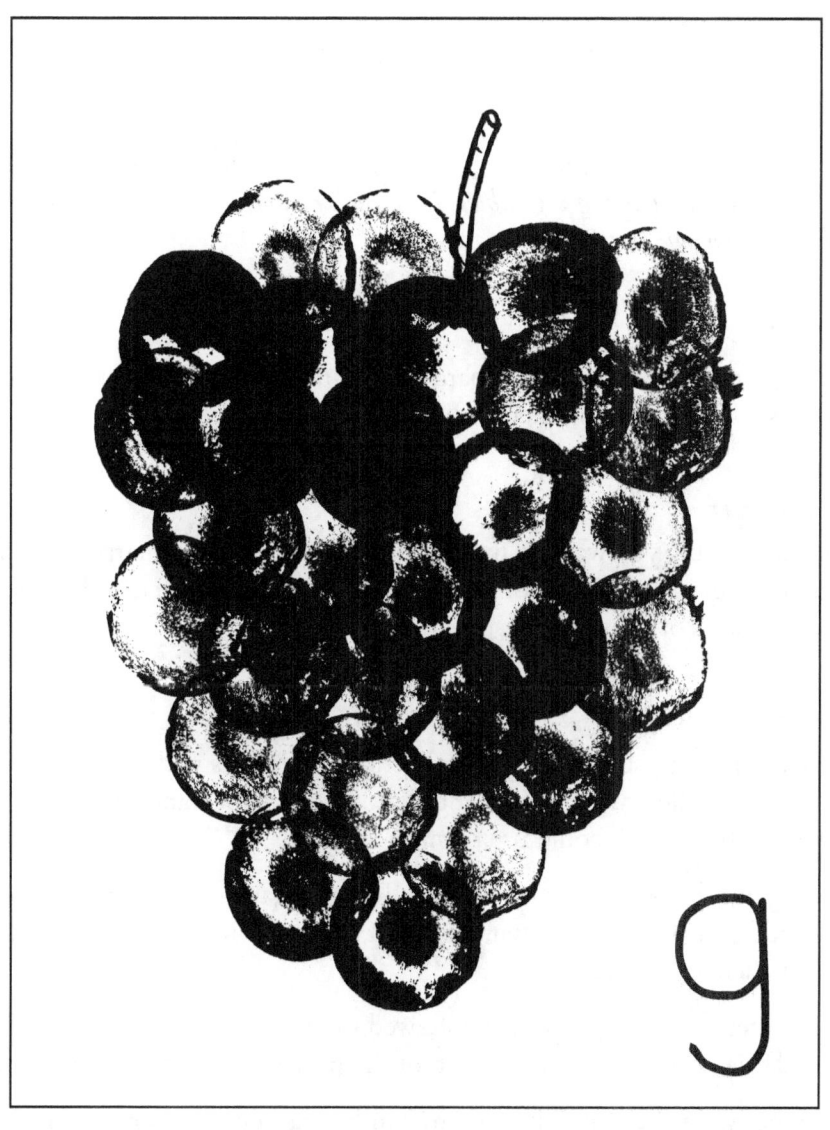

G

Plan a Garden

It's fun to plan a garden of one's own! While doing this activity, your child may become familiar with new varieties of vegetables. If so, include one or more in a meal and be sure to let her help you prepare it.

☞ What You Need:
Construction paper or poster board, seed catalogs or pictures of vegetables, scissors, glue, colored marker

✄ To Prepare:
Decide how big you want to make the garden. Use either a large sheet of construction paper, a piece of poster board, or tape or glue together four smaller sheets of construction paper.

☆ Activity:
1. Look through a seed catalog or collection of pictures with your child. Name the different vegetables and discuss their appearance, how they grow, and how you could use them in a meal.

2. Bring out the paper or poster board. Tell her that she is going to make a garden art piece of her own, a kind of map showing where she would grow each vegetable.

3. Have her say the word *garden*, followed by the first sound, *g*. Write your child's name and *garden* at the top of the project, pointing out the letter *g*.

4. Ask her what she would like to grow in her garden, then invite her to cut, arrange, and glue on vegetable pictures. Help as needed.

G

A Small Gift

A token of appreciation can brighten a person's day. Take a few minutes to help your child think about the important people in his life and on how he can show gratitude for their kindness and care.

☞ What You Need:
A small gift for each member of the family, wrapping or tissue paper, scissors, tape, paper, colored markers, pencil

☆ Activity:
1. Chat with your child about his family. Include close friends, if you wish. What makes each person special? How do they contribute to the family or to the community? Explain that giving gifts is a way to show that we appreciate and care about others.

2. Tell him that the word *gift* begins with the letter *g*. The word *giving* begins with *g* too. Have him say *g, gift* and *g, giving* a few times to highlight the sound. Write the letter and have him trace it with his fingers or with a pencil.

3. Together, think of a small gift for each family member. These may be handmade, purchased, or gently-used items.

4. Once the objects have been gathered, invite your child to carefully wrap each one.

5. Cut a large tag from plain paper. Write the recipient's name on the card with the word *gift*. Invite your child to decorate the tag with colored markers and attach it to the present.

6. Now ask her to give each person their gift, along with a few kind words about how much she appreciates them.

G

G Is for Glass

This activity includes a bit of scientific experimentation. It also sends your child on a search for glass in your home, which heightens her awareness of her environment.

☞ **What You Need:**
Paper, pencil, several identical drinking glasses, wooden chopstick or spoon, water

☆ **Activity:**

1. Invite your child to join you in the kitchen. Write the letter *g* on the paper and say its sound. Ask her to write the letter and say its sound several times.

2. Set out several drinking glasses. Point out that even though they are solid, we can see through them. Explain that this is because they are made of glass. Have her say *g, glass*.

3. Fill the glasses with different levels of water. Demonstrate, then invite her to gently tap them with the wooden spoon or chopstick. Notice the different tones that are produced.

4. Let her curiosity guide her experimentation with other containers, if she desires. When she is finished, remind her that *g* is for *glass* and ask her to find other glass items in your home, such as windows, mirrors, glass over pictures, eyeglasses, lamps, jewelry, television or computer screens, jars, cookware, bottles, or a fish tank.

G Is for Glass • 71

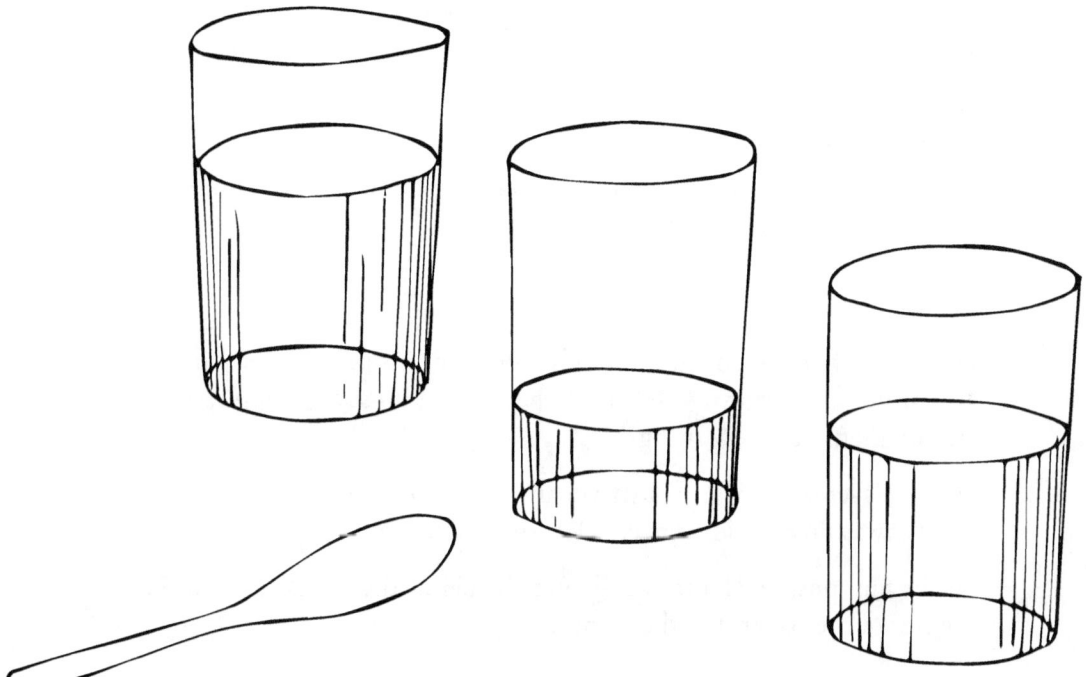

H

Hand Print Picture

After doing this project, make a collage on a large sheet of paper, including prints from all family members!

☞ **What You Need:**
Construction paper, poster paint, dishwashing liquid, disposable styrofoam tray or pie pan, glue, colored marker

☆ **Activity:**

1. Ask your child to look at his hands and count his fingers. Tell him that the word *hand* begins with the letter *h*. Have him say *h, hand* several times, then practice writing *h*.

2. Pour a layer of paint into a styrofoam tray or pie pan. Mix in a few drops of dishwashing liquid to make cleanup easier.

3. Have him push his hand firmly into the paint, then press it onto the center of the paper. Let the print dry.

4. Cut a frame from a second sheet of construction paper in a contrasting color and glue it over the print.

5. Write your child's name under the print. Add the date beneath. Introduce the capital letters for your child's name and the month if you wish, or write them using the lower case letters he is used to.

Variation:
For a simpler activity, trace around his hand with a pencil instead of making a paint print. Frame and label it as above.

Hand Print Picture

H

Heart Chain

Add a splash of color to a wall with this cut-and-glue project.

☞ **What You Need:**
Construction paper, scissors, colored pencils or markers, glue, tape

☆ **Activity:**
1. With your child, cut out a stack of construction paper hearts in different colors. Tell her that the word *heart* begins with the letter *h.* Together, say *h, heart* several times.

2. Demonstrate, then invite her to write an *h* on each of the hearts.

3. Again demonstrate, then have her glue the hearts top to bottom to form a chain. Let dry.

4. Tape the Heart Chain on a wall or make a bracelet from a short chain of small hearts.

Variation:
Attach pictures of individual family members on a wall. Have your child ask each person their favorite color, then build a heart chain of that color beneath the corresponding photo.

Heart Chain • 75

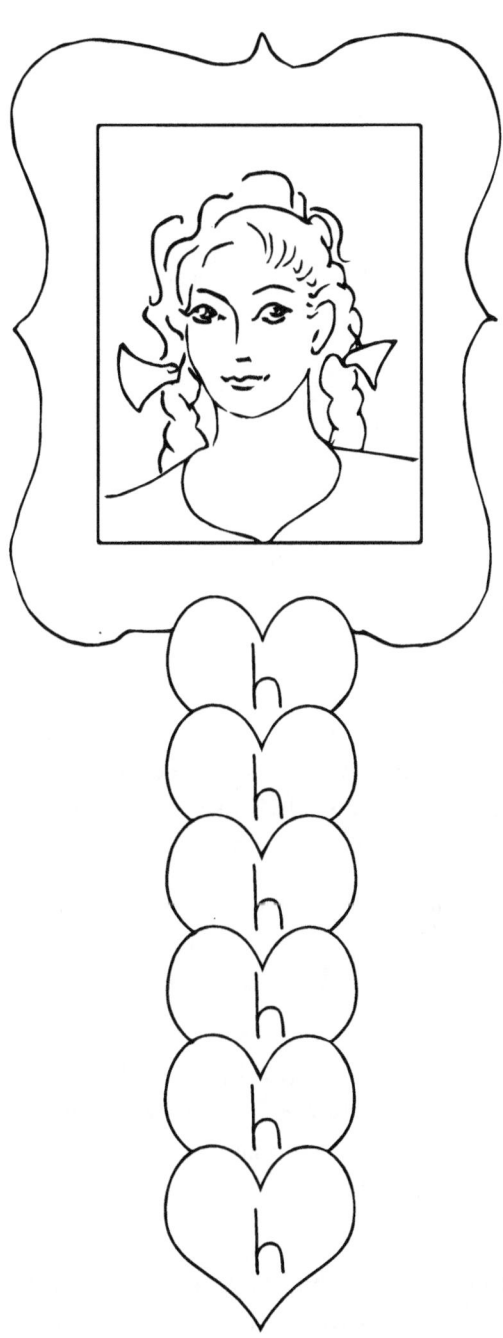

❧ H ❧

Hop! Hop!

Vigorous physical activity is important for health and aids learning. So hop to this fun lesson on the letter h!

☞ What You Need:
Pictures of animals that hop and those that don't, poster board, basket, marker, scissors, tape

✂ To Prepare:
1. Cut out pictures of various animals, some that can hop (kangaroo, rabbit, grasshopper, frog, robin, mouse, flea) and some that can't or generally don't (snake, fish, elephant, whale, worm, porcupine, bear, giraffe, snail). Mix up the pictures and place them upside down in a basket.

2. With marker, draw a line near the top of a sheet of poster board and write *hop* on it.

☆ Activity:
1. Tell your child that today he is working with the letter *h*. Explain that *h* is the first sound in these words: *hip, horse, head, hammer, hose, hair, hamster,* and *heart*. Say them together, emphasizing their first sounds. Now say that *h* is also the first letter in *hop*. Ask him to say *h, hop* while hopping for a bit.

2. Compliment him on his fine hopping, then ask if he can think of any animals that hop. After discussing this for awhile, bring out the prepared

poster board and tell him that he is going to make a display of those animals. Point out the first letter of the word *hop*. Set the board and tape at a distance.

3. Bring out the basket with the animal pictures. Invite him to choose one and think about whether the creature normally hops. If not, have him set it aside. If so, tell him to hop with the picture to the display and tape it on. Continue until all the animals have been sorted.

ℋ

H Is for House

Let your child's creativity guide her in building a house. Encourage her to expand on the basic construction by decorating the interior or adding a bit of landscaping.

☞ **What You Need:**
Building materials (blocks, Lego bricks, or sugar cubes), crayons, paper, craft sticks (optional)

☆ **Activity:**
1. Explain to your child that *h* is for *house* and *home*. Talk about the different types and sizes of dwellings that people live in: apartments, huts, houses, houseboats, mobile homes, etc. Discuss how these provide safe places for families to live together.

2. Bring out the blocks, Legos, or sugar cubes and tell her that she is going to build a house with the material. Say *h, house* together several times.

3. Invite her to build a house of her own design. If using sugar cubes, demonstrate how to set a slip of paper over a space between two cubes to form a window or doorway, providing a base for another layer. Add a flat roof by setting craft sticks on top, if desired.

4. Finally, write the letter *h* on a piece of paper and set it next to the structure. Invite her to add more *h*'s of her own, using different colored crayons.

H Is for House • 79

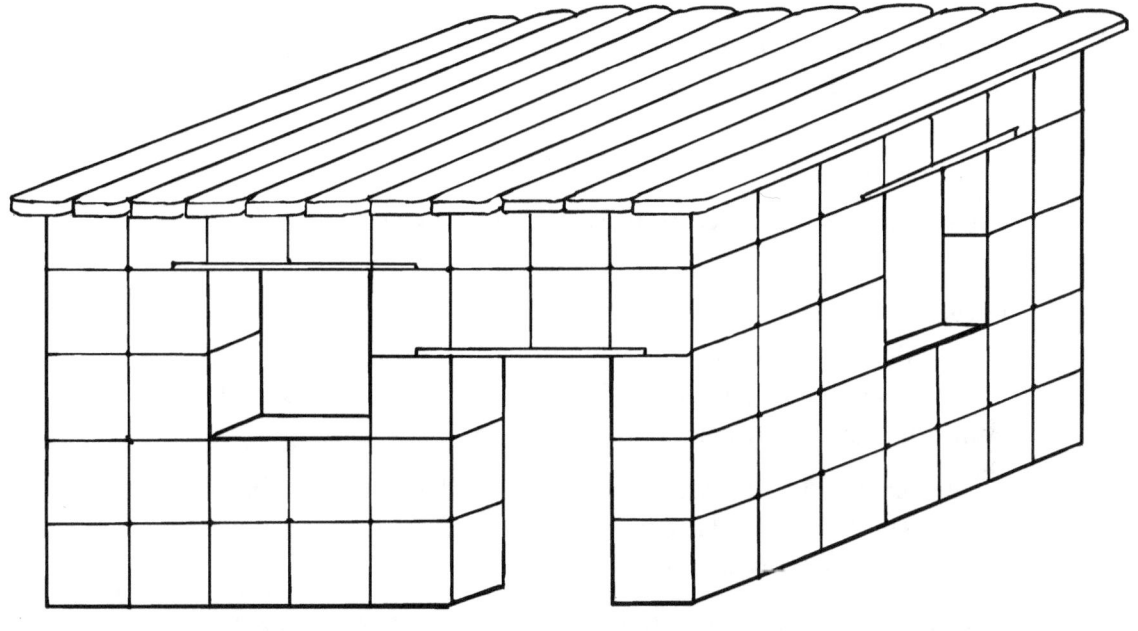

❦ I ❦

INSECT POSTER

Challenge your child to find as many pictures of strange and varied types of insects as can he can, and then display them on his poster.

☞ **What You Need:**
Construction paper, insect stickers or pictures, scissors, glue, colored marker

☆ **Activity:**
1. Begin this activity with a discussion of insects. Point out that they have a head, thorax, abdomen, and six legs. Look at pictures of assorted insects and name their body parts.

2. Tell your child that the word *insect* begins with the letter *i*. Together, say *i, insect* several times. Write the letter at the top of a sheet of construction paper; under it write the word *insect*.

3. Have him select, cut out, arrange, and glue pictures of insects on the paper to make his display. Let it dry.

4. Show him how to "tell the story" of his poster in this way: Point to the *i*, the word *insect*, and then one of the pictures. Say, for example, *"i, insect, grasshopper."* Ask him to repeat for each insect image until he has told the story for the entire poster.

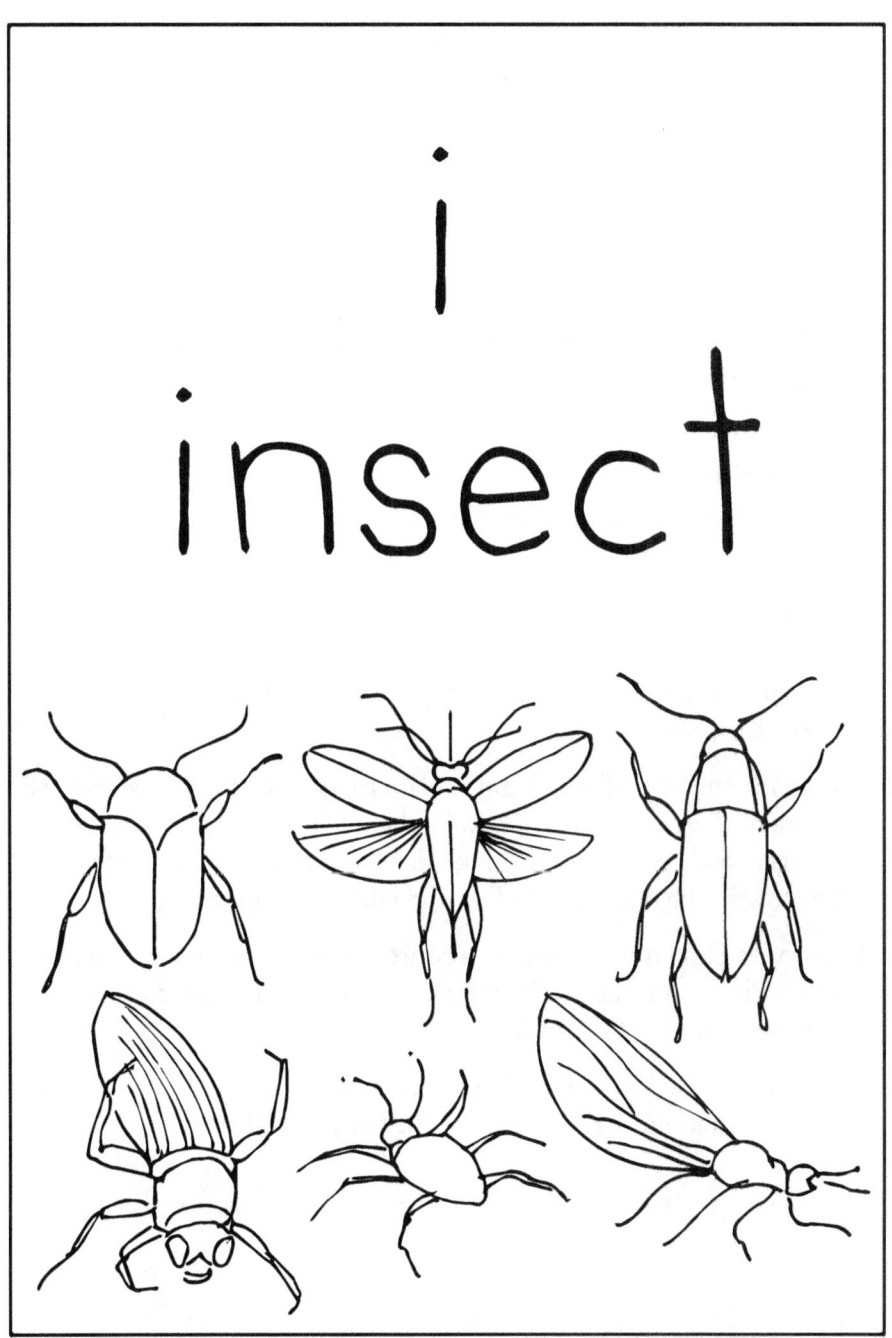

❦ 1 ❦

HOW MANY INCHES?

Once your child had collected information about the lengths of various items, show her how to organize the data on a chart.

☞ **What You Need:**
Paper, ruler, pencil, things to measure

☆ **Activity:**
1. Bring out the ruler and count the inches with your child. Point out the half inch marks and explain that they indicate the distance halfway between the inches.

2. Write *inch* on a slip of paper and explain that the word begins with the letter *i* and therefore, *i* is for *inch*. Ask her to trace over the letter with her fingers and say its sound. Make sure she traces it in the pattern it is written, with the down stroke first and ending with the dot.

3. Demonstrate, then invite her to measure items in your home, rounding either to the closest inch or half inch. As she does this, jot down the names and lengths of the objects.

4. Once you have a list, draw a simple bar graph and show her how to write in the information. Ask her to color the bars, as indicated.

How Many Inches?

	inches													
pencil	▨	▨	▨											
envelope	▨	▨	▨	▨	▨	▨	▨							
spoon	▨	▨	▨	▨	▨									
paperclip	▨													
cookie	▨	▨	▨											
	1	2	3	4	5	6	7	8	9	10	11	12	13	14

❦ I ❧

Iggy Iguana

Hide this reptile somewhere at eye level to give visitors a surprise!

☞ **What You Need:**
Cardstock, construction paper, glue, picture of an iguana

✂ **To Prepare:**
Draw and cut out an iguana shape from cardstock.

☆ **Activity:**

1. Look at the picture of an iguana with your child. Explain that iguanas are reptiles. They are big lizards that live in warm, dry places. Some people keep them as pets. They have four legs, a long tail, have spines down their back, and are covered with dry, leathery skin and scales.

2. Together, say *i* is for *iguana* several times. Bring out the prepared iguana shape and introduce it as Iggy Iguana.

3. Ask him to snip some construction paper into "scales." Then have him decorate the iguana by gluing them on.

4. Tape the finished project on the wall or set Iggy against a potted plant or picture in your home.

Iggy Iguana • 85

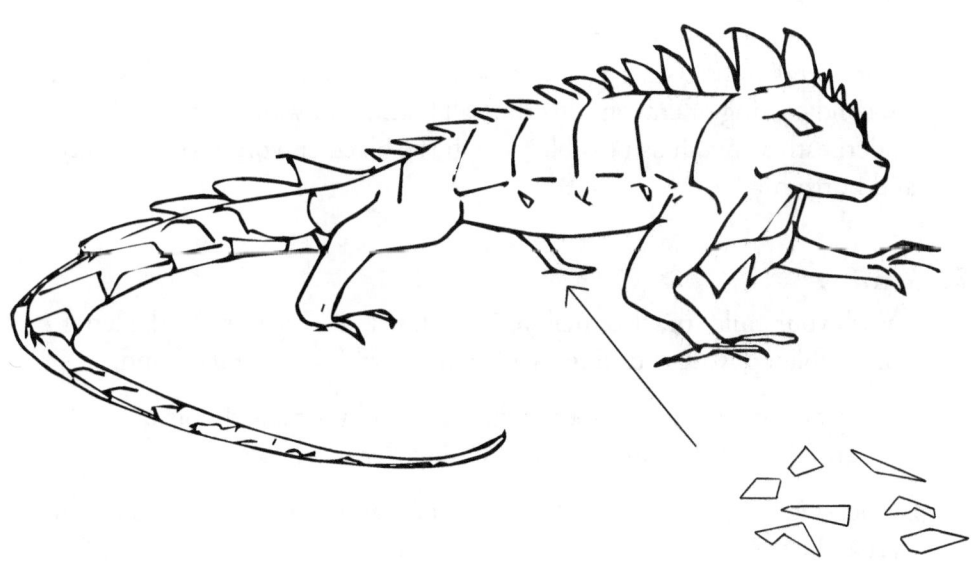

Colorful *i*'s

Each time a letter is scratched into the wax, colors bloom from beneath, revealing new patterns.

☞ What You Need:
Construction paper, thick crayons, wooden popsicle stick

✂ To Prepare:
Cover a half-sheet of construction paper with wide stripes of bright-colored crayon. Press hard to lay down a thick coating of wax. Now make a second coating of crayon, this time all black. You want to hide the colors underneath as much as possible, so rub the black crayon both vertically and horizontally.

☆ Activity:
1. With your child, practice making the "down, dot" pattern of the letter *i* on a tabletop with your fingers a few times while saying its sound.

2. Bring out the prepared paper. Invite your child to scratch lots of *i*'s into the surface with the popsicle stick to discover what colors are beneath.

3. When she is satisfied with the picture, congratulate her on her "Colorful *i*" art and hang it on a wall.

Colorful I's • 87

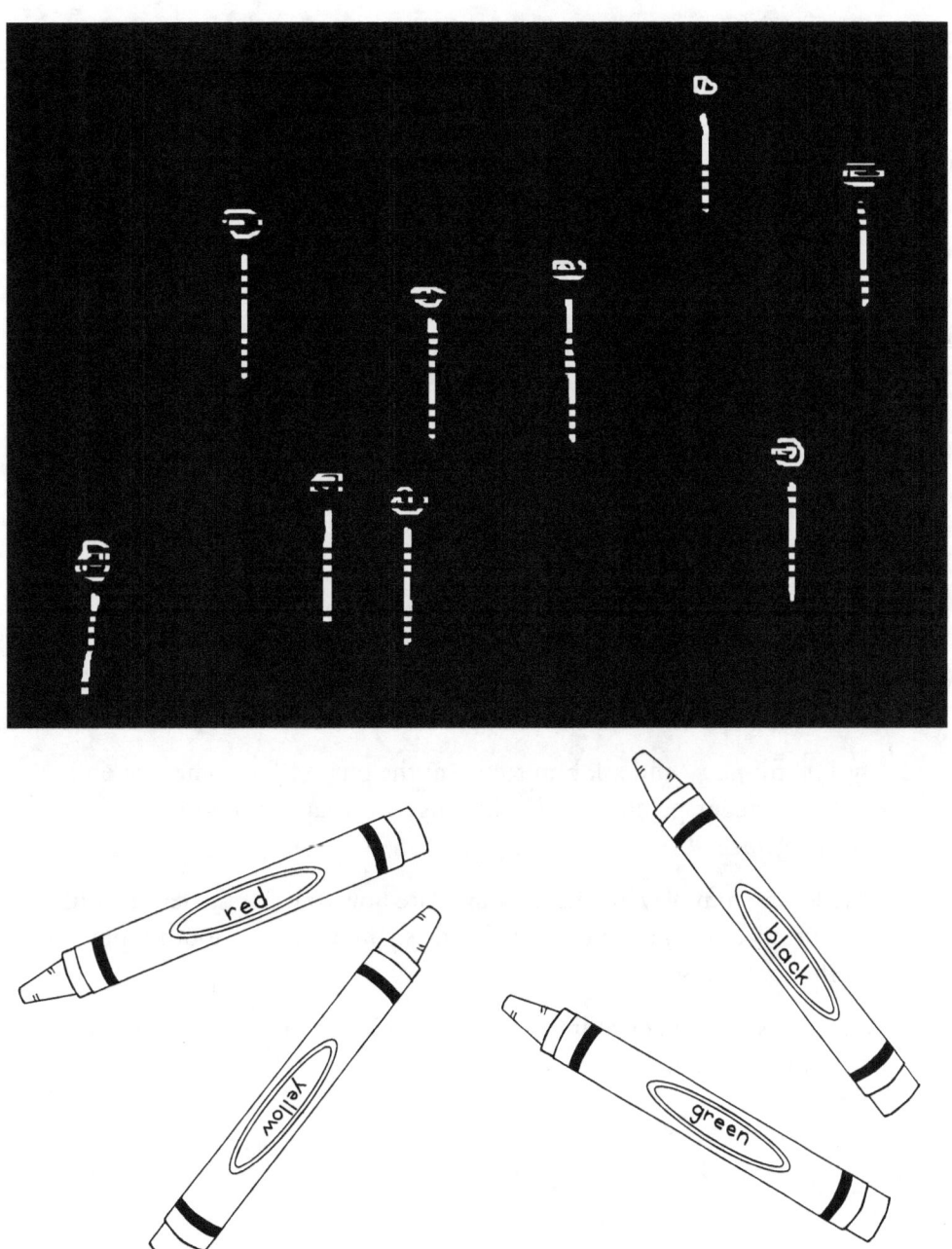

∽ J ∾

Jam Swirl

This tasty lesson engages all the senses. What a great way to learn the letter j!

☞ **What You Need:**
   Jam, plate, butter knife, bread

☆ **Activity:**
   1. Show your child a jar of jam and ask him what he thinks it is made of. Point out and say the name on the label. If, for example, it is strawberry jam, discuss how strawberries grow and how they are cooked with sugar to make the treat. Open the jar and smell it.

   2. Say, "*j* is for *jam*," and ask him to repeat the phrase. Put some jam on the plate and encourage him to swirl his fingers through it, smooth it, then swirl it again.

   3. After letting him play awhile, demonstrate how to write the letter *j* with your fingers in the goo. Say the *j* sound as you do this. Smooth it out and let him do it himself.

   4. When he is finished experimenting, invite him to spread some fresh jam on bread and eat it!

Jam Swirl • 89

J

Jeans and Jackets

One, two, three, four! How many jeans are in your drawer?

☞ **What You Need:**
Closet of clothes, construction paper, pencil, ruler, star stickers

✂ **To Prepare:**
Draw lines on two sheets of construction paper, as illustrated, adjusting your charts to the number of people in your home. Write *jeans* on the top of one sheet and *jackets* on the top of the other.

☆ **Activity:**
1. Practice saying the *j* sound with your child and have her practice writing the letter.

2. Explain that *j* is the first letter in *jeans* and *jackets,* and that she is going to see how many she can find in your home. Ask her to count her own clothing and then write down the numbers. Help as needed.

3. Now have her ask other members of the family to count their jeans and jackets or let her count them. Jot down these numbers as well.

4. Once the data are collected, show her how to chart the information using sticker stars to indicate how many items each family member has.

jeans

	1	2	3	4	5	6	7	8	9	10	11	12	13	14
amy	☆	☆	☆											
mom	☆	☆	☆	☆	☆	☆	☆	☆						
dad	☆	☆	☆	☆	☆									
kyle	☆	☆	☆	☆										

jackets

	1	2	3	4	5	6	7	8	9	10	11	12	13	14
amy														
mom														
dad														
kyle														

J

A Pen Jar

Everyone needs a way to organize their writing tools. This pretty homemade container gets the job done!

☞ **What You Need:**
Small to medium-sized wide-mouth jar, paper, pencil, colored tissue paper, small paintbrush, glue, styrofoam tray, marker, glitter (or colored sand) and plate (optional)

☆ **Activity:**

1. Set out the jar and explain that *jar* begins with *j*. Write the letter on paper, then have him practice writing it and saying its sound a few times. Explain that he is going to decorate the jar to make a pen and pencil holder.

2. Ask him to tear some of the tissue paper into quarter-sized pieces.

3. Pour glue into the styrofoam tray. Demonstrate how to brush a thin layer of glue over a patch of glass and then apply pieces of brightly-colored tissue paper. Invite him to continue the process until the entire jar is covered.

4. Optional: While the project is still damp, have him roll the jar in glitter (or colored sand) that you've sprinkled on a plate, brushing on extra glue, if needed. This step requires extra supervision so he doesn't get any glitter in his mouth or eyes. Have him wash his hands immediately when finished.

5. Set the jar aside to dry overnight. The next day, review the *j*'s sound with him, then suggest he fill the container with pens, pencils, or markers.

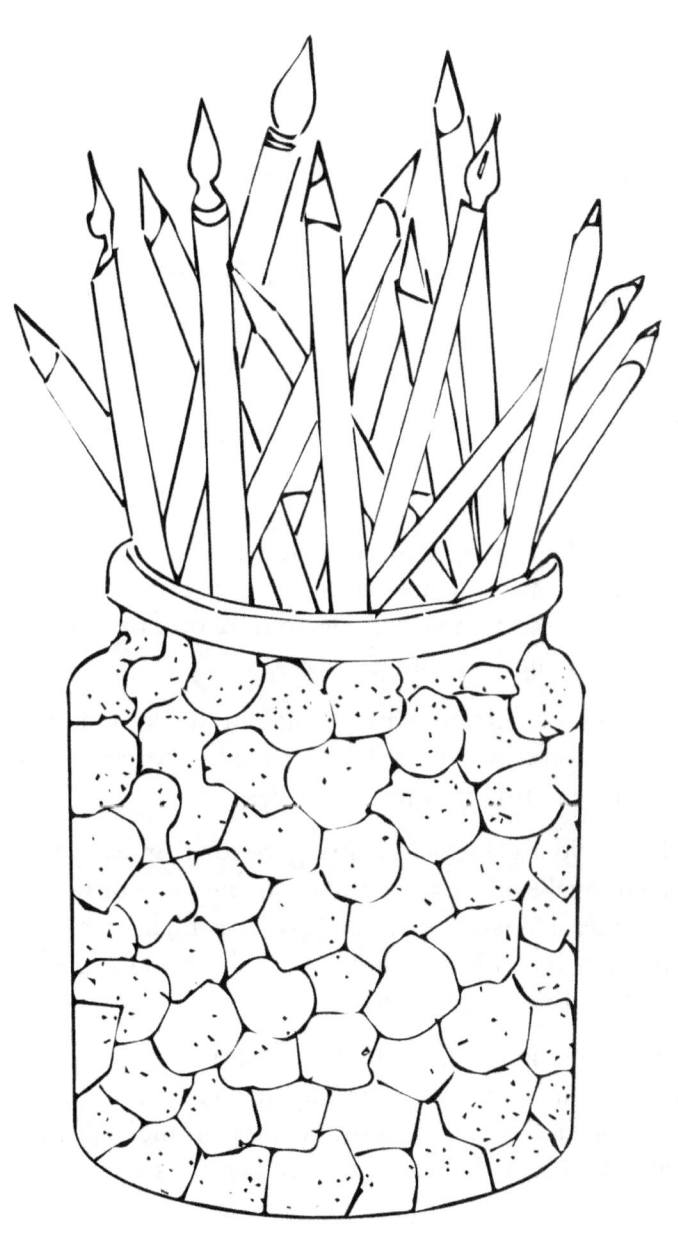

J

Jet Game

Let your child's imagination soar while becoming acquainted with another letter.

☞ What You Need:
Paper, pencil

☆ Activity:

1. With your child watching, print large letters *j*, *e*, and *t* on a piece of paper. Say the sound of each letter as you write it. Have her practice saying *j* is for *jet*. Next, show her how to trace over the *j* (down and curve, then make a dot) and write more of her own.

2. Explain that jets are airplanes that fly high in the sky and that you are going to play a game where you both pretend to be jets. She is a fast little jet, while you are the big mama or papa jet.

3. Begin piloting your planes while sitting together. Spread your arms wide and pretend to take off. Begin with her "flying" at your side while you both remain seated. Say, "I spy, from my jet so high . . . a _____." Name a small portable object in your home and ask her to fly to get it and bring it to you. Repeat with other items.

4. When she has brought you a collection of things, compliment her on her excellent flying and say, "We're running low on fuel, so we'll have to land soon. Can you take each item home before you land?" When all have been replaced, circle the house once with her, arms spread wide, then "land," sitting on a sofa, chair, or on the floor.

5. Conclude the activity by briefly reviewing the letter *j*.

Jet Game • 95

K

Kite on the Wall

After doing this project, watch for a breezy day when you can teach your child how to fly a real kite!

☞ **What You Need:**
   Construction paper, tape, scissors, glue, colored pencils or markers

☆ **Activity:**

1. Say, "*k* is for *kite.*" Have your child say *k, kite* several times. Discuss what kites are and explain that he is going to make a decorative kite to hang on the wall.

2. Use construction paper to build the body of the kite, making it smaller or larger as you desire. Invite him to decorate it creatively, then attach it to a wall or bulletin board.

3. Ask him to help you cut several tail pieces from assorted colors of construction paper.

4. Now demonstrate how to write the letter *k* and say its sound. Have him write lots of *k*'s on the tails, using different colored pencils or markers. Let his interest guide the activity. He might want to write all the *k*'s at once or do one tail per day.

5. Attach the *k* tails to the kite as they are completed.

Kite on the Wall • 97

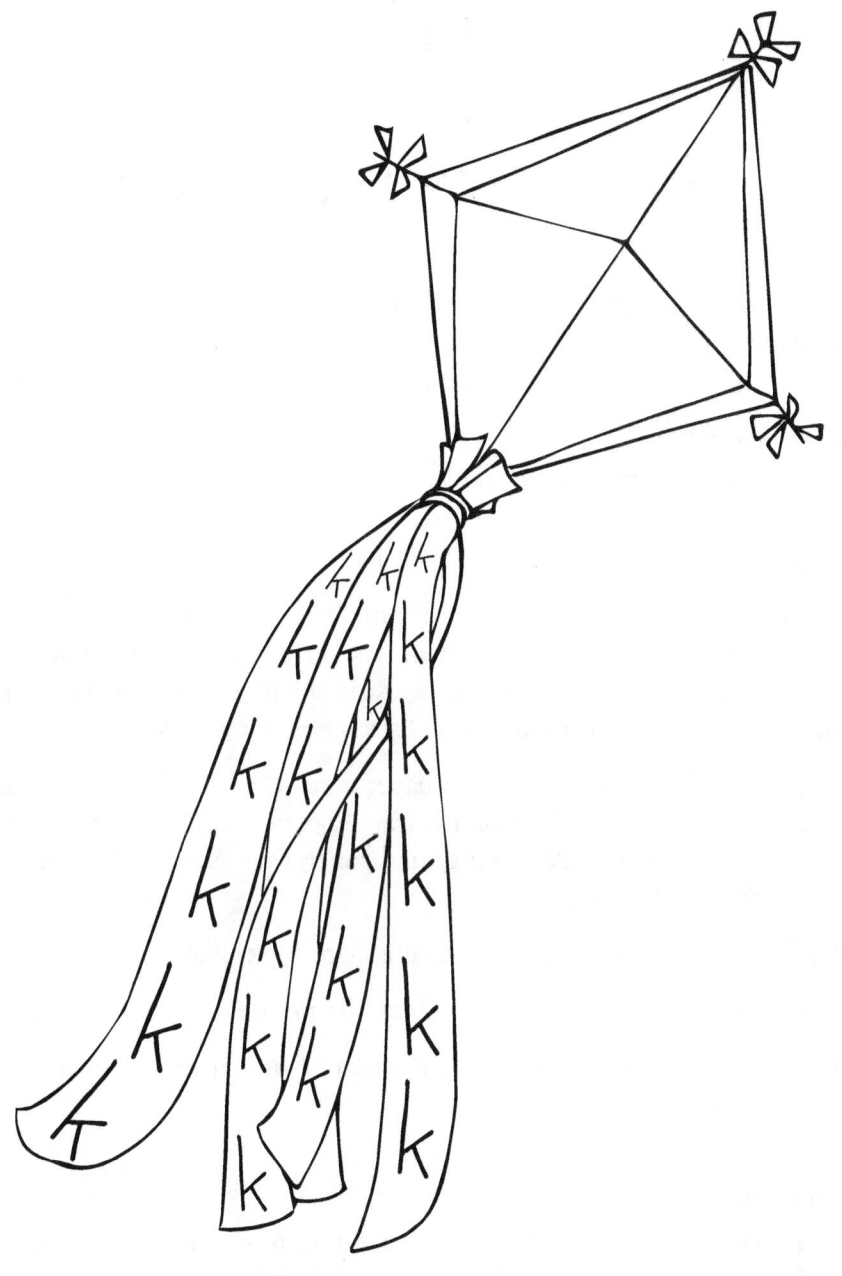

❦ K ❦

Fun with Ketchup

Blob pictures are amusing to make and interpret. Ask friends what they see in the abstract designs!

☞ **What You Need:**
Ketchup, construction paper, tray

☆ **Activity:**
1. Set out a bottle of ketchup. Point out the letter *k* on the bottle and have your child say *k, ketchup* a few times. Ask her if she knows what ketchup is made of, then invite her to taste it. Read the ingredient list aloud and note that it begins with tomatoes. Discuss how they grow.

2. Cut several sheets of construction paper in half. Fold each piece in half, like notecards, and set them on the tray. Ask your child to squirt a blob of ketchup onto one side of a prepared paper, then press the two sides together to squish the sauce.

3. Unfold the paper and discuss what the shape looks like.

4. Encourage her to make lots of ketchup pictures herself. Let them dry.

5. Demonstrate, then have her write the letter *k* on her favorite pieces and display.

Variation:
Squirt ketchup onto a large sheet of paper or onto the tray. Invite your child to finger paint with the sauce. After playing for a short time, show her how to form *k* in the ketchup. Cheer her on as she makes more of her own.

Fun with Ketchup • 99

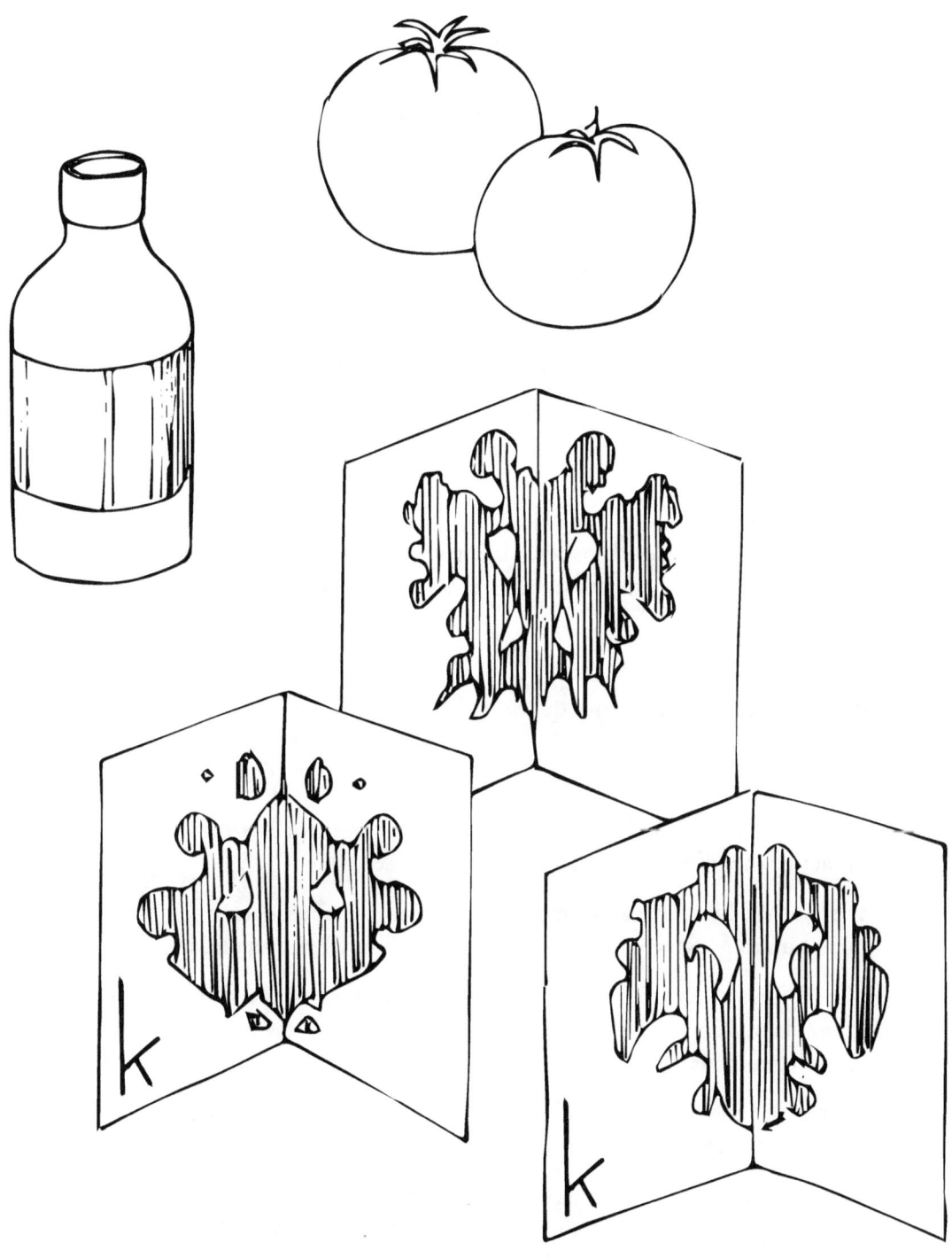

K

A Book of Keys

Keys come in many interesting shapes and sizes, from old fashioned skeleton keys to dainty ones made for jewelry boxes. This lesson explores these variations and guides your child to create a booklet of his discoveries.

☞ What You Need:
Keys of various sizes and shapes, plain paper, thick crayons with paper removed, pencil, construction paper, scissors, stapler

✂ To Prepare:
Cut five sheets of paper into quarters.

☆ Activity:

1. Introduce the lesson by telling your child that *k* is for *key*. Have him practice the phrase. Discuss what keys are used for.

2. Set out the keys, one at a time, inviting him to inspect each one carefully. Ask him to guess what they open, then tell him what they unlock.

3. Demonstrate how to place a piece of paper over a key and rub firmly with the side of a crayon to make the shape appear. Encourage him to make lots of rubbings of his own.

4. Have him choose the ten rubbings he likes the best. Form the sheets into a book by stapling them between two construction paper covers.

5. Finally, show him how to write the letter *k* with pencil, then have him practice printing it and saying its sound. When he feels confident, have him write a *k* on each page of the booklet, facing the rubbing.

A Book of Keys • 101

6. At a later time, have him "read" you the book by pointing to the *k* and saying its sound, and then pointing to the key and saying what type it is. Here are some examples: *k, car key; k, lock box key; k, post office box key; k, jewelry box key; k, house key; k, padlock key;* etc.

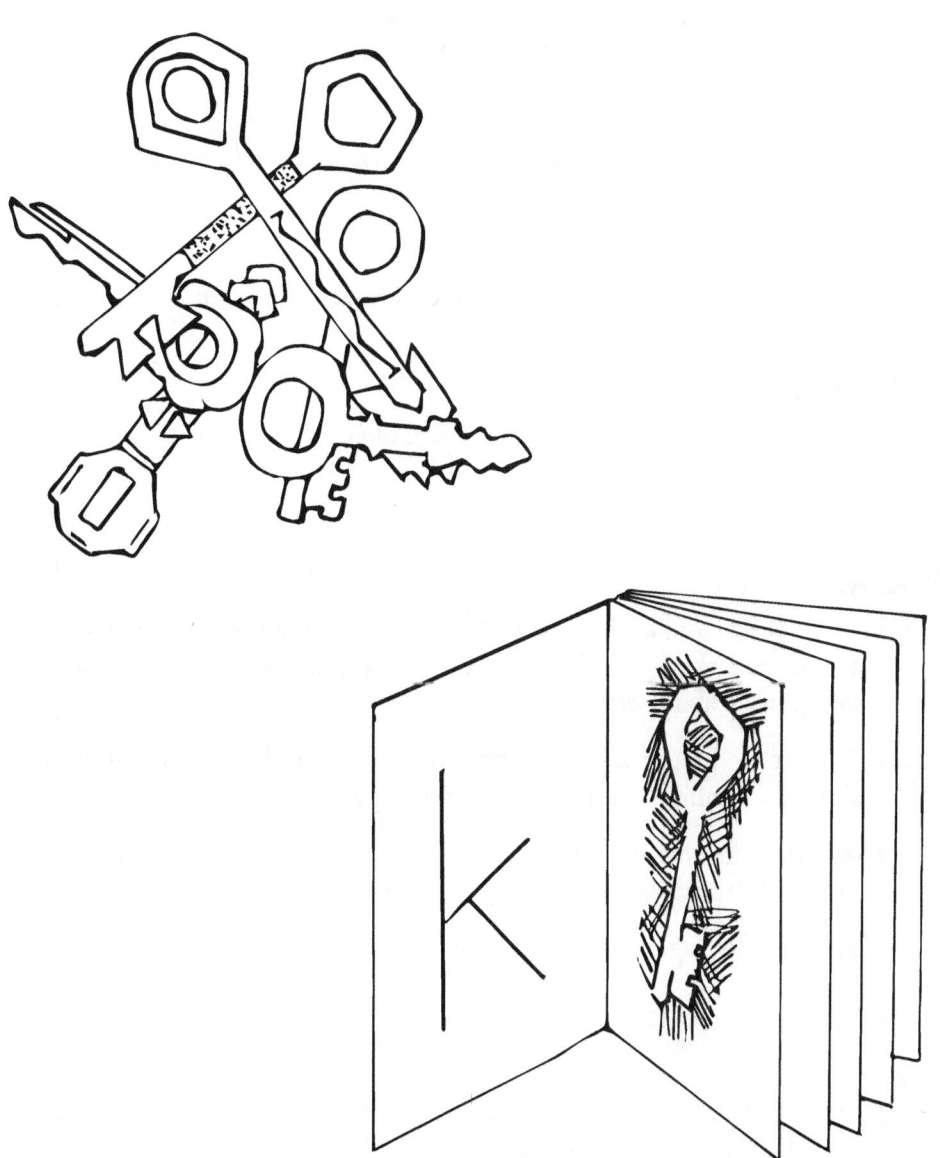

K

Popcorn Kitty

If your child has any stuffed cats, have her gather them to "watch" her do this art project.

☞ What You Need:
Popcorn, construction paper, plain paper, glue, marker, pencil

✀ To Prepare:
1. Draw an outline of a large cat on a piece of construction paper.
2. Pop the corn.

☆ Activity:
1. Sit with your child and say that today she is working with the letter *k*. Have her practice saying its sound and writing it. Ask her to listen for the *k* sound in *kitty* and *kitten*.
2. Bring out the prepared cat outline. Invite her to add eyes, nose, mouth, and whiskers, and then write a *k* on the page and say *k* is for *kitty*.
3. Now bring out the bowl of popped corn and invite her to glue pieces all over the illustration to make a Popcorn Kitty!
4. When dry, display where she can greet the kitty often.

ℒ

Lemonade

Mmm! Everyone appreciates a glass of chilled lemonade on a hot summer day.

☞ **What You Need:**
Lemons, sugar, water, glass, spoon, paper, pencil

☆ **Activity:**

1. Write a large *l* on a piece of paper and say its sound. Have your child trace it and make more of his own.

2. Bring out a lemon and explain that *l* is for *lemon*. Invite him to smell and taste it. Which end was attached to the tree it grew on? Cut it crosswise and note the inner sections. Does it have seeds?

3. Explain that its juice makes a tasty drink, but it needs a bit of sugar to make it less sour. Proceed to make the recipe below together, letting him do as much as possible. Adjust the sweetness according to taste and the tartness of your fruit.

Lemonade

Step 1
In a quart jar, stir $^1/_2$ cup sugar into 2 cups warm water until dissolved. Let cool.

Step 2
Stir in:
1 cup freshly squeezed lemon juice
3 cups cold water

Put a few ice cubes in your prettiest glasses, then pour in the lemonade. Add a sprig of mint or a lemon slice, if desired.

Variation:

Follow the recipe, substituting limes for lemons.

L

Watercolor Leaves

Leaves are such a common sight that it's easy to forget that they are complex, energy producing, and alive! This project is a great introduction to the subject.

☞ What You Need:
Assorted leaves, construction paper, tape, watercolor paints, paintbrush, jar of water, newspaper

☆ Activity:

1. Take a walk with your child to collect a variety of different sized and shaped leaves.

2. Spread out the leaves and look at them, noting their differences and similarities. Have her find their central and side veins. How do their borders differ? Explain that leaves convert the energy of sunlight into food that plants use to live and grow.

3. Say, "*l* is for *leaves.*" Have her repeat the phrase, then show her how to write *l*. Ask her to print it at the top of a sheet of construction paper.

4. Set the sheet on a stack of newspapers. Demonstrate how to tape leaves on the construction paper, brush over them with watercolor, then set the page aside to dry. Invite her to make more of her own, writing an *l* at the top of each new piece.

5. When the art is dry, remove the leaves to reveal the leaf-shaped designs.

Watercolor Leaves • 107

~ L ~

MISS LADYBUG

Learn more about this helpful, colorful insect with this fun art project!

☞ **What You Need:**
Construction paper, scissors, glue, black marker, pictures of ladybugs, black pipe cleaner (optional), book on insects (optional)

☆ **Activity:**
1. Look at pictures of ladybugs (observe a live one, if you can) and learn about their life cycle. Observe that different species have varied coloration and numbers of spots. Note that, like all insects, they have six legs. Also, they all have three body parts (head, thorax, abdomen). The soft thorax is hidden beneath a hard plate called *pronotum*. And the soft abdomen is hidden beneath the wings and their hard coverings called *elytra*.

2. Have him say *l, ladybug* a few times. Ask him to trace a *down* motion with this hand on a sheet of construction paper, then have him write the letter at the top.

3. Together, cut out and glue an orange and black ladybug on the paper. Glue on two short lengths of black pipe cleaner (or paper) for antennae.

4. Attach the picture to a wall. Encourage him to say "*l* is for *ladybug!*" when he shows it to friends.

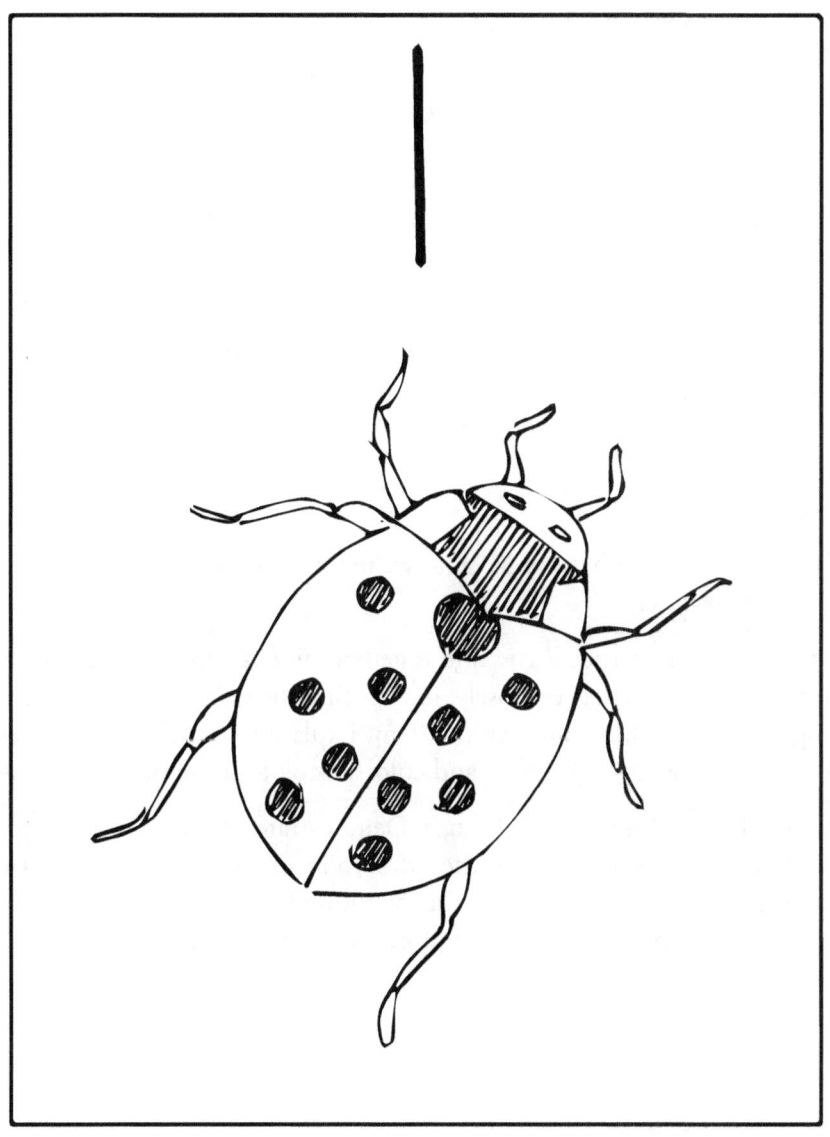

L

LETTUCE WRAPS

Serve this tasty, healthy snack the next time you need an appetizer.

☞ What You Need:
Paper, pencil, washed lettuce leaves, pictures of assorted varieties of lettuce, spoon, plate, filling of your choice (cottage cheese, bean dip, tuna salad, nut butter, sliced fruit, cheese, or meat)

☆ Activity:

1. Demonstrate, then have your child write lots of *l*'s, saying the letter's sound each time.

2. Bring out some lettuce leaves and together say *l, lettuce* a few times. Invite her to examine the leaves closely, first tracing the veins and edges with her fingers, then smelling and tasting them. Explain that different varieties of lettuce have varied leaf shapes and colors. Look at some pictures of them.

3. Now bring out one or more fillings. Demonstrate how to put a spoonful of filling in a lettuce leaf, fold in the sides, roll it up, then set it on a plate. If the leaves are brittle, then just put the filling in the center and don't roll them. Let her make more wraps of her own, then munch and enjoy!

Lettuce Wraps • 111

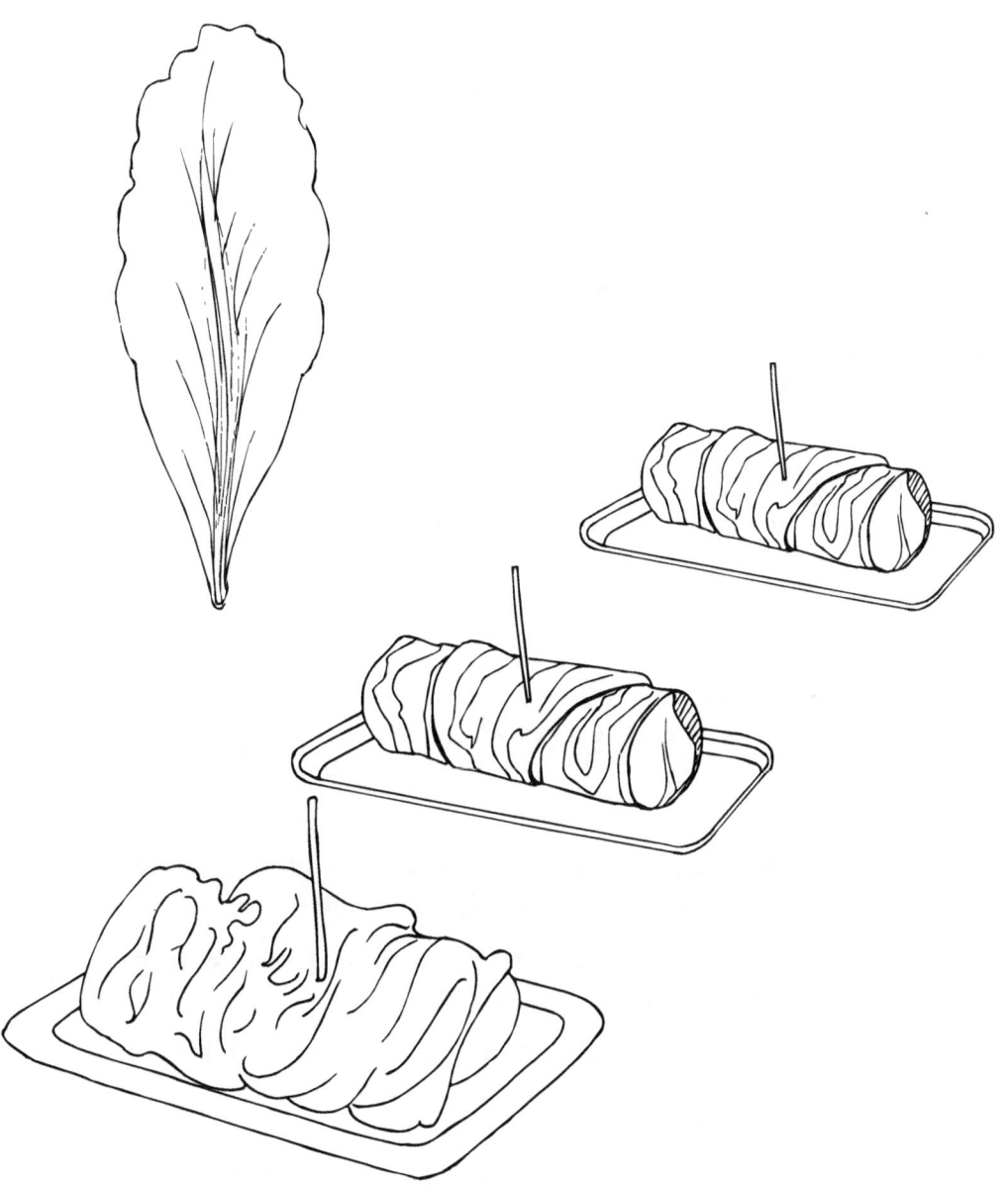

∽ M ∽

Mustard Squirt

There are many ways to practice making letter shapes. Here's a fun project that you can adapt for other letters. Try it with numbers, too!

☞ **What You Need:**
Yellow mustard in squirt bottle, large piece of paper or plastic tablecloth (optional)

✂ **To Prepare:**
Fill a half empty squeeze bottle of prepared mustard with water, diluting it until you get a consistency that's easy to squirt.

☆ **Activity:**
1. Announce that you are doing a really fun project with the letter *m*. Say, "*m* is for *mustard.*" Have your child chant *m, mustard* a few times.

2. Bring out the bottle of mustard. Make sure the lid is secured, then ask him give it a vigorous shake.

3. Now show him how to write the letter *m* with the mustard. Do this outside on snow or sand, in a bathtub or shower, on a large piece of paper, or on a plastic tablecloth.

4. After practicing writing a few *m*'s, invite him to draw designs of his own.

Mustard Squirt · 113

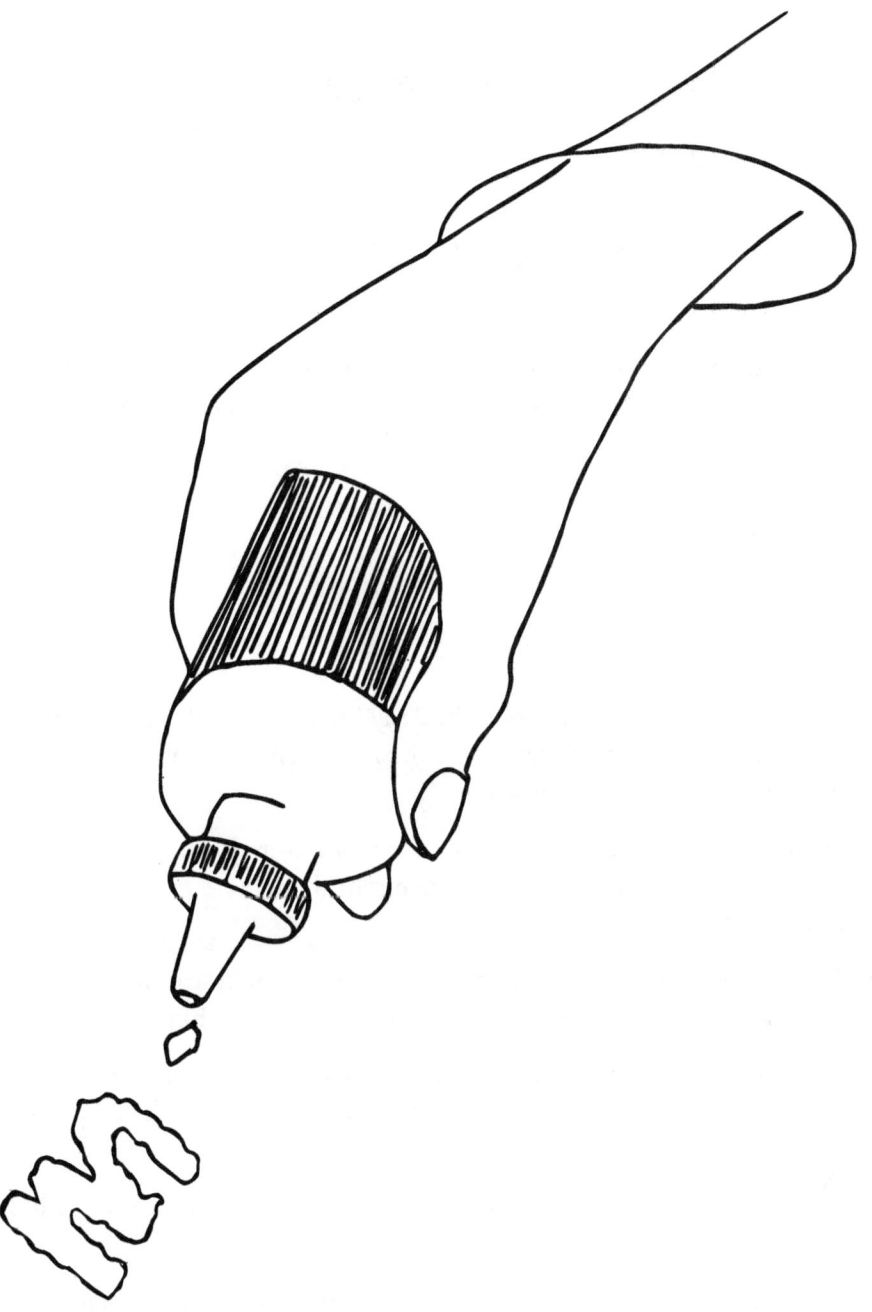

~ M ~

Treasure Map

Making and reading this map is an early exercise in thinking abstractly and translating the world into symbolic form. If your child doesn't have a room of her own, simply follow these steps in another area.

☞ What You Need:
Paper, pencil, small treat or gift

☆ Activity:

1. Say, "*m* is for *map*." Have your child say *m, map* several times. Explain that a map is a drawing that shows the important areas of a place. Today she will make a map of her room.

2. Demonstrate how to write *m* (down, up and over, down, up and over, down) and say its sound. Encourage her to write more *m*'s, saying the sound each time.

3. Together, look around her room and discuss its main features. Guide her in drawing a simple outline of the room and its furnishings.

4. Let a bit of time pass. When you notice that she is busy in another part of the house, hide the small treat or gift in her room. Mark the map with an X to show where it is hidden.

5. Now show her the X on the map. Explain that it marks the spot of hidden treasure and ask her to find it.

6. If desired, repeat this lesson with more complicated maps or make a hunt where one map leads to another until ultimately revealing the treat.

～M～

Mushroom Mobile

Decorate your home with a collection of colorful mushrooms while introducing your child to the fascinating world of fungi.

☞ **What You Need:**
Construction paper, scissors, crayons or colored markers, glue, string or yarn, hangar or two sticks, a real edible mushroom, mushroom pictures

☆ **Activity:**

1. Say, "*m* is for *mushroom.*" Have your child say *m, mushroom* several times. Show him a real edible mushroom and encourage him to use all his senses to investigate it. Point out the cap, stem, and gills.

2. Look at pictures of other types of mushrooms. Tell him that some are good to eat, but others are very poisonous. He should never eat, or even touch, a wild mushroom that he finds outside unless he is given permission by an adult who knows it is safe.

3. Together, cut construction paper mushroom caps and stems. Write a few *m*'s on the caps. Suggest he decorate them using crayons or colored markers, or by gluing on snips of paper.

4. Punch a hole in each mushroom top and tie on a piece of yarn or string. Tie the pieces to a hanger (or two sticks tied together in the middle to form an X), varying the lengths so the mushrooms hang at different levels.

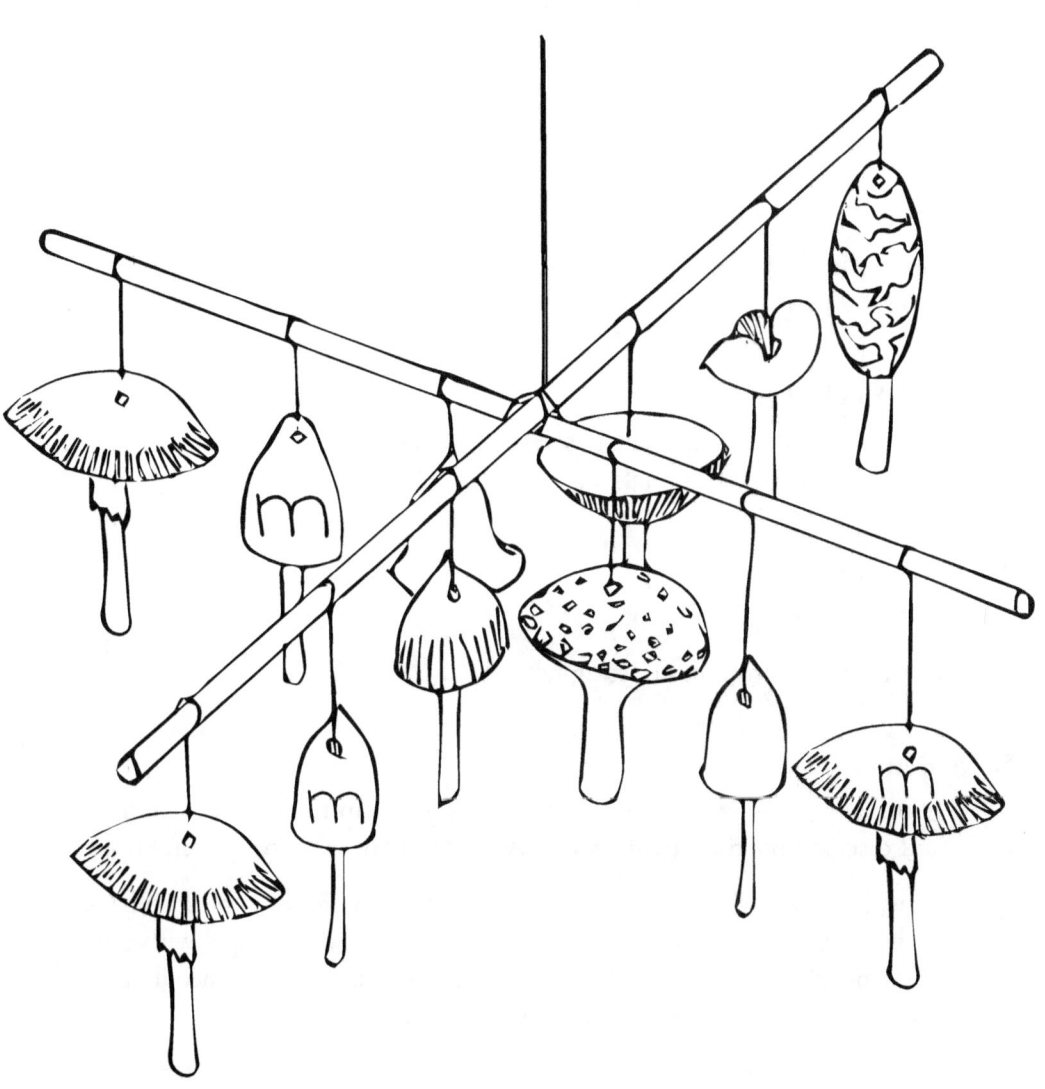

M

Felt Mitten

Simple up and down sewing is fun and helps develop muscular control. Try making these cute mittens as holiday ornaments.

☞ **What You Need:**

Felt, scissors, blunt craft needle, safety pins, yarn, glue, waxed paper, pair of gloves and mittens (optional)

✂ **To Prepare:**

1. Cut two mitten shapes from felt.

2. Cut a letter *m* from contrasting felt.

☆ **Activity:**

1. If available, show your child a pair of gloves and mittens. Compare them and discuss how they are different. Ask her to say *m, mitten* several times.

2. Show her the two prepared felt mitten shapes. Secure them back to back with safety pins. Begin to sew them together around the edges with the blunt needle and yarn. Work slowly to demonstrate how the needle goes up and down. Let her complete the project as she is able.

3. Bring out the felt *m*. Show her how to trace the letter with her fingers, then ask her to glue it onto the mitten. Lay a sheet of waxed paper over the project, then press under a heavy book until dry.

4. The next day, have her trace over the felt *m* once more and say its sound, then display.

Felt Mitten • 119

N

N Is for Neck

This lesson opens a world of exploration. What is inside a neck? And why do we and other animals have them? The activity also includes an introduction to measuring and comparing large and small.

☞ **What You Need:**
Pictures of animals, measuring tape, paper, pencil

☆ **Activity:**

1. Ask your child to point to his neck and yours. Discuss what purpose his neck serves. It holds up his head (and allows him to turn it), connects his mouth with his stomach (with a tube called the esophagus), contains his windpipe (which allows him to breathe), and holds his vocal chords (which allow him to sing, speak, and yell). There is a lot going on inside a neck!

2. Bring out the paper and pencil and show him how to write the letter *n* and say its sound. Have him practice this a few times.

3. Together, look at pictures of animals—such as a giraffe, a dog, and a mouse—and ask him to find their necks and comment on their similarities and differences.

4. Bring out the measuring tape and point out the inch and half-inch marks. Then have him measure his neck, your neck, and those of several other people (and pets, if you have any). Together, write down each measurement and then find out whose neck is largest and smallest.

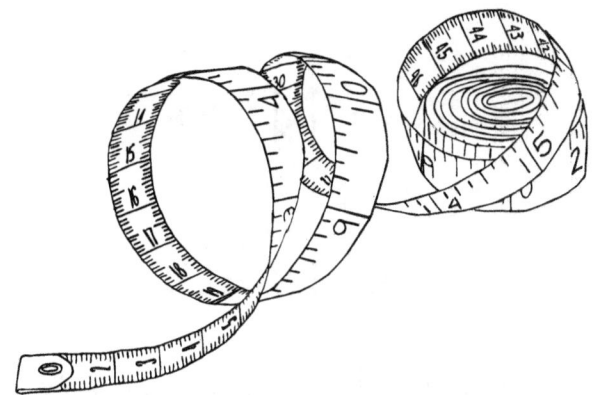

dad <u>15½</u> inches

mom <u>12</u> inches

rose ___ inches

jack ___ inches

N

Necklace

When your child wears this necklace, the letter n *is unmistakable. Everyone she meets will reinforce the lesson by commenting on it.*

☞ What You Need:
Paper, pencil, colored markers, bowl of uncooked tubular pasta, yarn, glue, scissors

✂ To Prepare:
1. Cut a length of yarn about three inches longer than you need to make a necklace.
2. Wet two inches of one end with glue and let dry. This will stiffen the end, making it easier to string through the pasta.

☆ Activity:
1. With your child watching, write the letter *n* on a piece of paper and say its sound. Invite her to write lots of *n*'s, saying its sound each time.
2. Bring out a bowl of uncooked tubular pasta. Form a large letter *n* with the pieces. Again say its sound. Mix up the pieces and have her repeat your actions.
3. Together say, "*n* is for *necklace.*" Loop the unglued end of yarn through and around a piece of pasta and tie to secure. Demonstrate how to string pasta onto the yarn, then let her complete the project. Cut off the stiff glued end and tie the yarn together to form the necklace.

4. Write an *n* on a small piece of paper. Punch a hole at the top and tie it onto the center of the necklace with a bit of yarn. Suggest she decorate the pasta with colored markers and then wear her project. She might even like to make another for a friend!

N

Nutshell Prints

Dip and press. This satisfying activity is perfect in the fall, when nuts are plentiful. Of course if your child is allergic to nuts, skip this project.

☞ **What You Need:**

Whole walnuts, pecans, hazelnuts (also called filberts), Brazil nuts, and/or almonds; nutcracker, poster paint, styrofoam tray or pie pan, construction paper

Note: Peanuts are legumes. Pistachios and cashews are classified as seeds, not nuts. And although true nuts are also the seeds of the plants they grow on, the proper name of the group is nuts. Isn't language fun?

☆ **Activity:**

1. Set out the nuts and invite your child to examine them. Tell him that they grow on trees and are, in fact, the trees' seeds. Open a nut and have him look at what's inside. Say, "*n* is for *nut*" and have him say *n, nut* several times. Suggest he eat the nut.

2. Set out a sheet of construction paper and write an *n* at the top.

3. Pour some paint into the styrofoam tray or pie pan. Take an empty nut shell half (or a scrap of shell) and dip it in the paint, then press it onto the paper. Invite him to fill the sheet with nutshell prints. Let dry.

4. Ask him to add some *n*'s to the picture, then display the art where he can admire it.

Nutshell Prints • 125

N

Noodle Nests

Here's a quick lunch or dinner idea that is educational too!

☞ **What You Need:**
Spaghetti or linguine noodles, water, salt, bowls, olive oil or butter, hard-boiled eggs (shelled), paper, pencil, tossed green salad (optional)

☆ **Activity:**

1. Invite your child to make Noodle Nests with you. Say, "*n* is for *noodle* and *n* is for *nest*. Have her repeat this with you. Discuss how birds make nests to protect their eggs and young.

2. Cook the pasta in salted water according to package directions. While the noodles are cooking, show her how to write the letter *n* and encourage her to write lots of them.

3. Drain the pasta and toss it with olive oil or butter. Add salt to taste. When cooled to a safe temperature, have her divide the noodles into individual bowls, then place a hardboiled egg into the center of each to form nests.

4. Serve immediately along with a tossed green salad (optional).

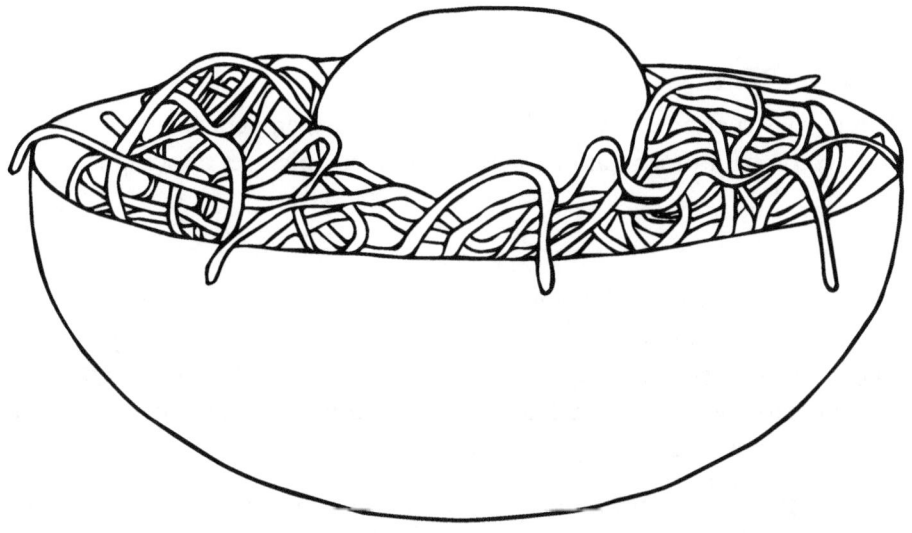

O

Octopus Picture

Introduce your child to these strange sea creatures with this simple art project.

☞ **What You Need:**
White construction or watercolor paper, plain paper, pencil, crayons, blue watercolor, paintbrush, jar of water, newspapers, pictures of octopuses

☆ **Activity:**
1. Say, "*o* is for *octopus.*" Ask your child to say *o, octopus* several times. Tell him that octopuses are smart animals that live in the ocean. They have eight arms, big eyes, a beak, and three hearts. And they can change their skin color! Some are as small as your hand, others longer than a car. Look at pictures or videos of the creatures.

2. Demonstrate, then ask him to practice writing the letter *o* with pencil on a sheet of plain paper.

3. Now using crayon, have him write an *o* in a corner of a piece of white construction paper, then draw a large octopus. Tell him to press hard with the crayon to lay down a thick coating of wax.

4. Lay the paper on a pile of newspapers and have him brush a light-blue watercolor wash over the picture. The octopus will suddenly look like it is underwater.

5. Suggest he make another piece, adding a seaweed vine or a fish.

6. Let the Octopus Pictures dry flat, then display.

❦ O ❦

Olive Appetizers

This nutritious snack is fun to make and yummy to eat!

☞ **What You Need:**
Two or more types of olives, paper, pencil, toothpicks, cubes of cheese, plate

☆ **Activity:**

1. Say *o* is for *olive*. Have your child say *o, olive* several times. Set out the olives. Encourage her to look at, touch, and taste them, then describe her observations. Tell her that they are the fruit of the olive tree and that while many are eaten whole, vast quantities are pressed to make olive oil.

2. Demonstrate how to write the letter *o*. Point out that it is round like an olive. Invite her to write lots of *o*'s, saying its sound each time.

3. Explain the procedure, then invite her to make a plateful of appetizers by pressing a toothpick into the bottom of an olive, then pressing the other end of the toothpick into a cube of cheese.

4. Suggest she share the Olive Appetizers at the next family meal.

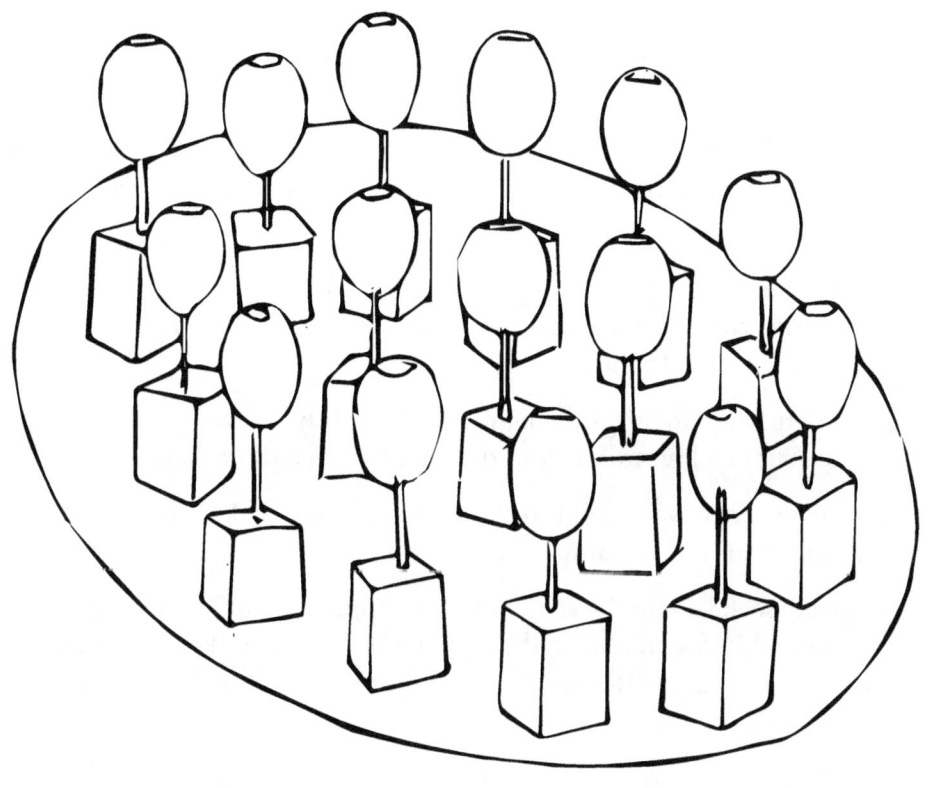

⊱ O ⊰

Octopus Doll

This doll happily sits on a shelf as a reminder that o *is for* octopus!

☞ **What You Need:**
Yarn, old sock, stuffing (craft stuffing, cotton, or rags), felt, scissors, glue

☆ **Activity:**
1. Invite your child to make an Octopus Doll with you. Together, say, "*o* is for *octopus*," several times.

2. Cut a large handful of yard long pieces of brightly-colored yarn. Lay the bundle out in a line and tie it in the middle with a short piece of yarn.

3. Meanwhile, have your child stuff the end of an old sock with craft stuffing, cotton, or rags to form a ball shape for the octopus's head.

4. Place the sock ball on the center of the laid-out yarn and fold the yarn up and around it. Secure the head by tying it off (at the neck) with a short piece of yarn. Adjust the strands around the sock ball to hide it. Cut off the excess sock.

5. Divide the loose yarn under the head into eight sections. Braid each section to form the legs, having him help as he is able. Tie off the ends with short pieces of yarn.

6. Cut out felt eyes and mouth. Have him glue on the features. Ask him to say *o* is for *octopus* once more, then find his octopus a home.

Octopus Doll • 133

O

Octagon Prints

This lesson introduces geometric shapes with different numbers of sides, along with some new vocabulary.

☞ **What You Need:**
Paper, pencil, two new cellulose sponges, scissors, poster paint, two styrofoam trays or pie pans, construction or watercolor paper

☆ **Activity:**
1. Draw a triangle. Say, "A triangle has three sides." Count the sides with your child, "One, two, three." Draw a rectangle. Say, "A rectangle has four sides." Together count, "One, two, three, four." Continue drawing and counting the sides of five-, six-, seven-, and eight-sided figures (pentagon, hexagon, heptagon, and octagon, respectively).

2. Say, "The word *octagon* begins with the letter *o.*" Have her say *o, octagon* several times. Demonstrate, then encourage her to write many *o*'s, saying its sound each time.

3. Pour two colors of poster paint into two styrofoam trays or pie pans. Cut two sponges into octagons.

4. Using one sponge for each color, demonstrate how to dip and print onto watercolor or construction paper. Invite her to make lots of pictures herself. Let dry, then display her favorites.

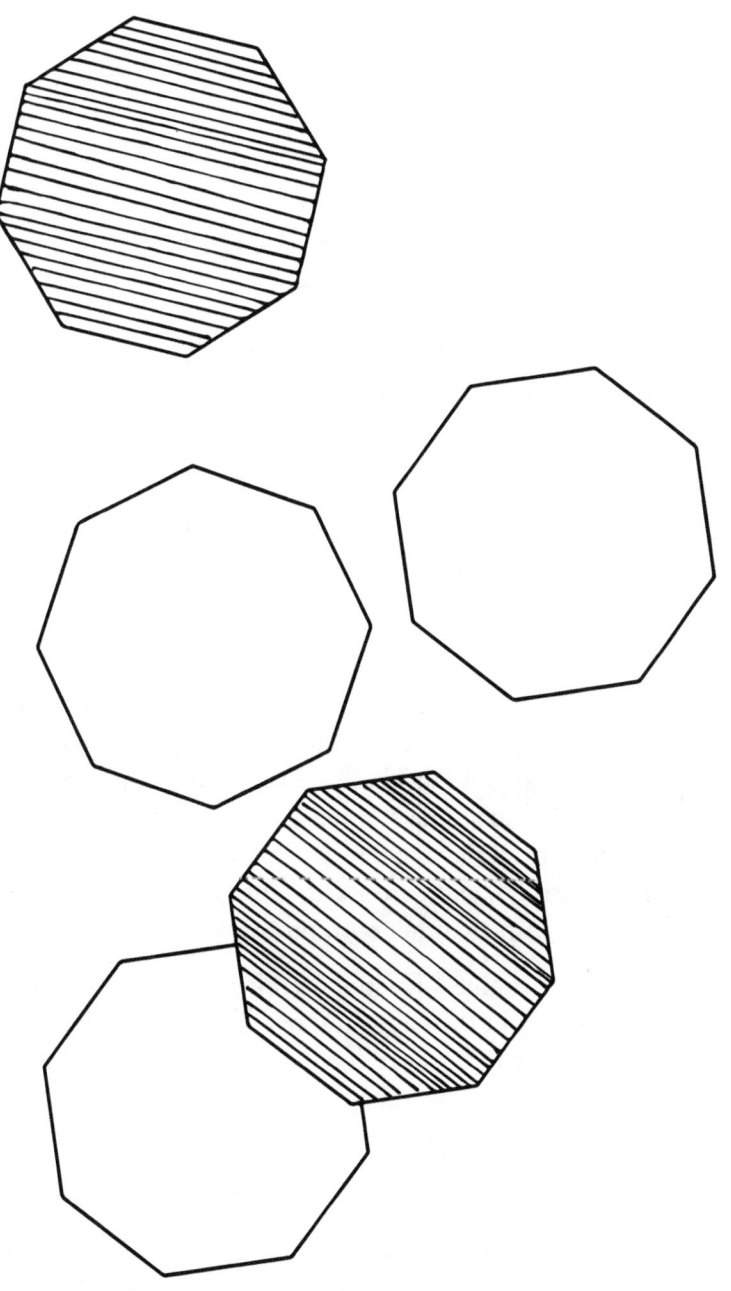

～ P ～

Popcorn Necklace

Stringing popcorn is a great exercise to improve both hand-eye coordination and fine motor control, important skills for writing.

☞ What You Need:

Paper, colored pencils, unpopped popcorn, popcorn machine or microwave oven, bowl, butter and salt, sturdy thread, large blunt craft needle

☆ Activity:

1. Introduce the activity by saying *p* is the first letter in *popcorn.* Have your child say *p, popcorn* several times. Tell him that popcorn is the seed of a large grass, corn. Explain that there are many different types of corn. Some varieties are fed to animals, some are eaten fresh, and some are dried and ground into cornmeal, which is used to make muffins, taco shells, breakfast cereal, tortillas, and cornbread. Corn oil, frozen and canned corn kernels, and corn syrup are other corn products.

2. Together, carefully examine a few popcorn kernels. Next arrange them into a *p* shape. Bring out the paper and pencils and show him how to write the letter. Say its verbal cue: down, up and around. Invite him to write lots of *p*'s with different colors.

3. Pop the popcorn and set a portion aside. Season the remainder with butter and salt, and invite him to eat some. Have him wash his hands.

4. String the blunt needle with a necklace-length double strand of sturdy thread and knot the end. Demonstrate, then let him string the unseasoned popcorn. Supervise his use of the needle closely.

5. Ask him to write a *p* on three rectangles of paper. Sew a short length of thread through the top of each paper and tie them to the necklace. Invite him to wear his fun necklace for a while, then put it outside for the birds to enjoy!

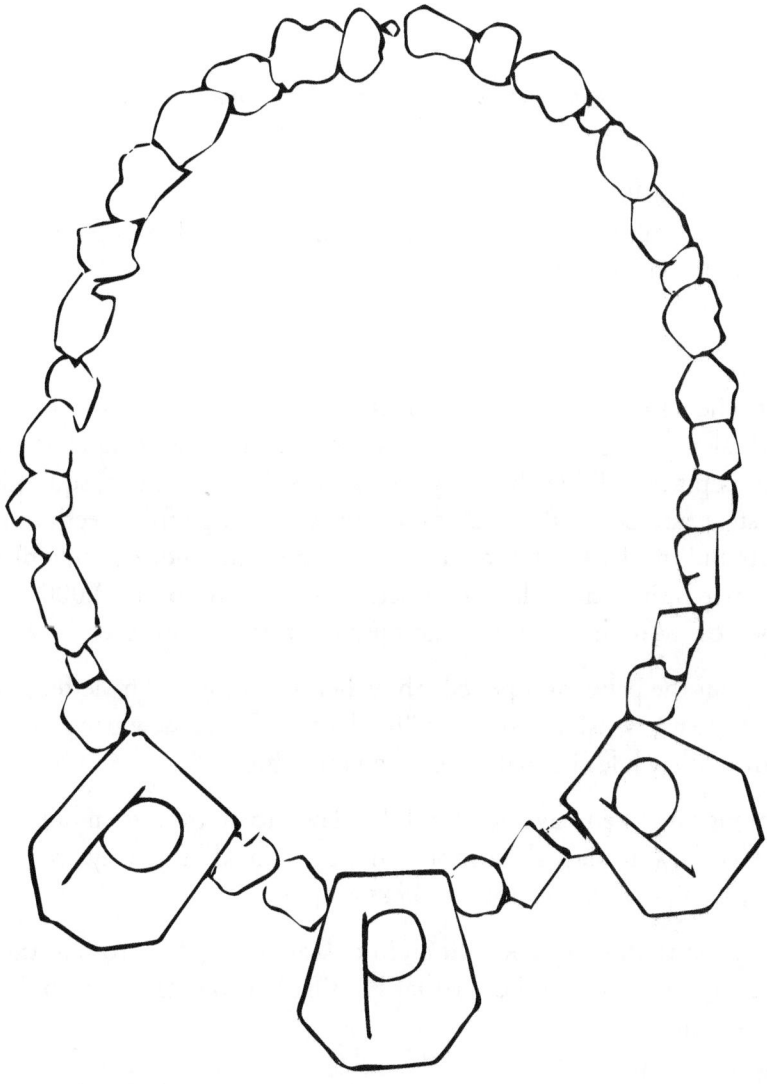

P

PEG THE PORCUPINE

Here is one animal that you don't want to get in an argument with!

☞ **What You Need:**
Pictures and online videos of porcupines, paper, pencil, modeling clay (or any sort of moldable material), toothpicks

☆ **Activity:**
1. Begin the lesson by saying that *p* is the first letter in *porcupine.* Have your child say *p, porcupine* several times. Look at pictures and watch videos of porcupines. Tell her that they are rodents (like mice, rats, squirrels, hamsters, and beavers), which means they have large front teeth to gnaw plants and tree bark. They are herbivores, meaning they eat only plants. Baby porcupines are called porcupettes. Adults have over 30,000 sharp spines, called quills, that they can raise to protect themselves.

2. Bring out the paper and pencil. Show her how to write the letter *p*. After practicing a few, ask her to write "her best one" on a new page and keep it on the table while she makes Peg the Porcupine.

3. Demonstrate, then have her mold the clay into an oval, then pull a bit of material forward to make a snout. Invite her to add two tiny eyes at the front, then press in lots of toothpicks as quills.

4. When Peg is finished, ask your child to search the house to find the perfect hiding place for her, perhaps setting her to peek out from behind a leafy plant!

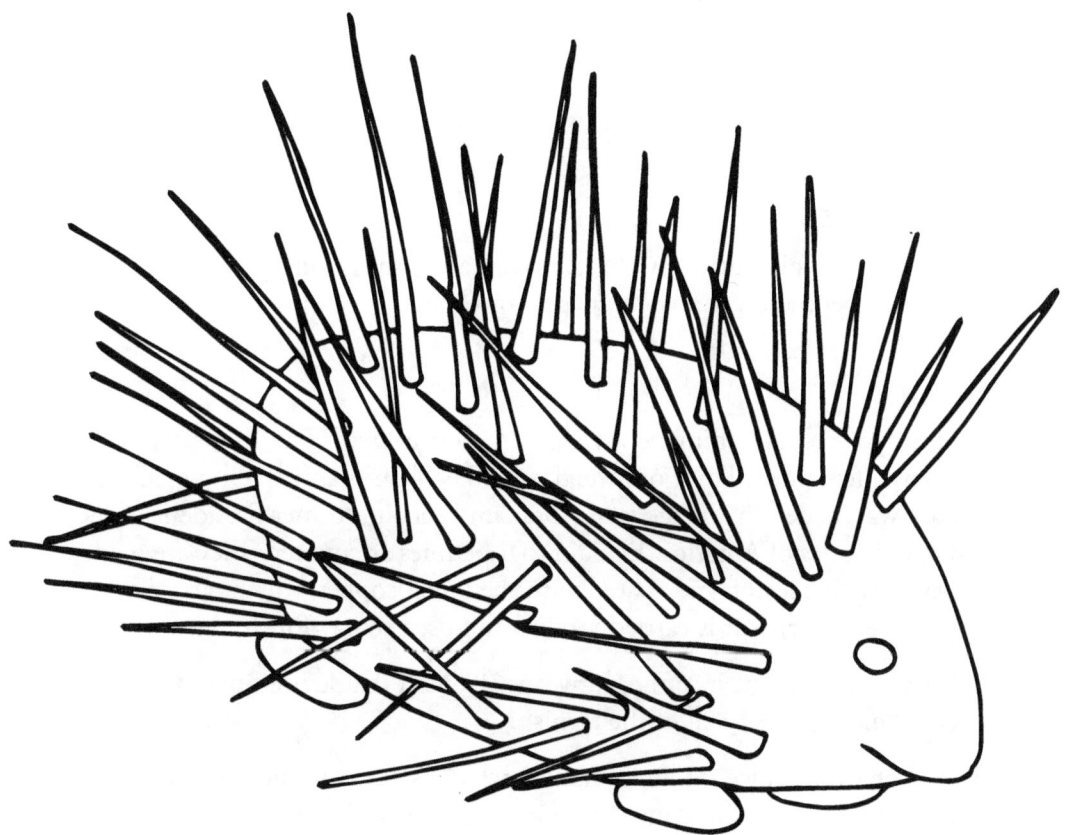

P

POLISH A PENNY

Watch the magic of acid and salt return the luster to tarnished pennies.

☞ **What You Need:**
Lemon juice, salt, cotton swabs, 2 small bowls, shiny penny, several tarnished pennies, warm water, paper towel

☆ **Activity:**

1. Show your child a shiny penny. Say, "*p* is for *penny.*" Have him say *p, penny* a few times. Point out the date and explain that this tells when the coin was made. The image is of Abraham Lincoln, former President of the United States of America. Explain that pennies are money. They are made from the metal zinc and coated with the metal copper, which tarnishes (changes color) as it is carried around and used to pay for things.

2. Set a dull penny next to the shiny one. Explain that lemon juice and salt can remove some or all of the tarnish.

3. Put the lemon juice into one small bowl and salt in another. Ask him place a tarnished penny into the juice and let it sit for half a minute or so. Instruct him to dip the end of a cotton swab into the juice, then into the salt, then remove the penny with his fingers and polish it with the salt-covered swab. Give the paste a few moments to work, then rinse the penny under warm water and dry with a paper towel. Admire its color. Let him polish more coins, if he desires.

P

PLACEMAT

If your child really likes this project, suggest she make a set of mats for the whole family.

☞ What You Need:

Two sheets of 9- by 12-inch construction paper, plain paper, waxed paper, clear contact paper, pencil, scissors, ruler, glue

☆ Activity:

1. Write a large *p* on a piece of paper. Have your child trace the letter with her fingers and say its sound several times.

2. Say, "*p* is for *placemat*. Today, you are going to make a placemat for the table." Have her practice saying *p, placemat.*

3. Ask her to choose two colors of construction paper. Fold the first piece in half, short end to short end. Measure, mark, and then cut eight lines (one inch apart) through the folded edge—stopping one inch from the outer edge.

4. Measure, mark, and cut the second sheet of paper widthwise (the short way across) into ten 1-by 9-inch strips.

5. Open the first paper. Demonstrate, then have her weave the strips over and under through the openings.

6. Have her put a dab of glue on each end. Press to secure. Place the mat between two sheets of waxed paper, then let it dry under a stack of books.

7. Cover the placemat with contact paper and invite her to use it at the next meal.

Placemat • 143

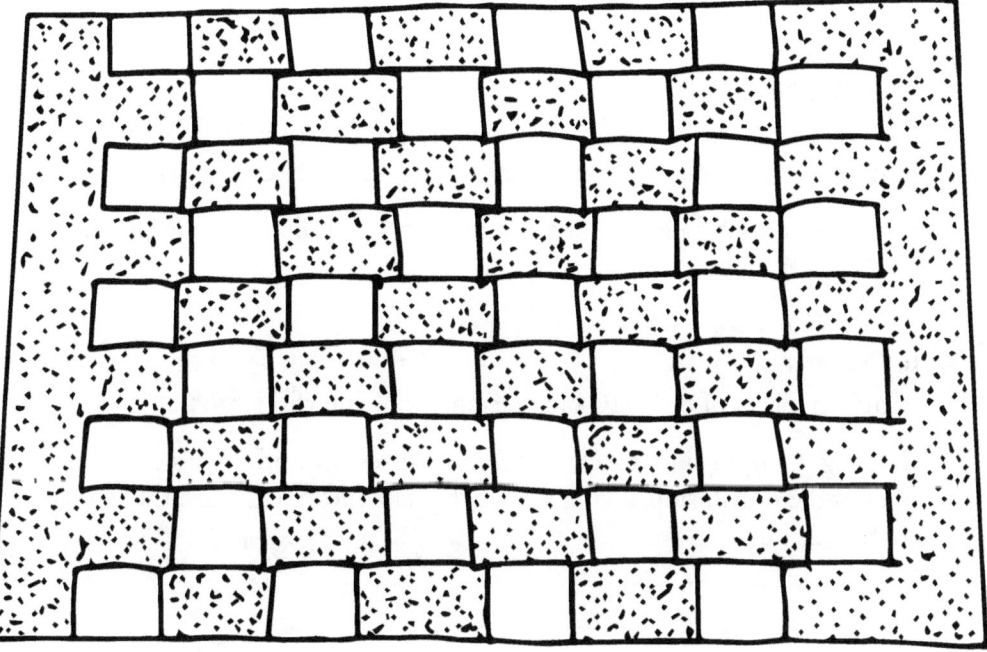

Q

QUILT

This colorful project is a lovely introduction to sewing. The finished quilt makes a pretty wall decoration or cover for a small table.

☞ What You Need:

Colorful fabric, thread, needle, craft stuffing or cotton balls, ruler, yarn, chalk or washable marker, blunt craft needle, scissors, sewing machine

Note: If you don't have a sewing machine, visit a quilt or sewing supplies shop and ask if someone can stitch up this little piece for you.

✂ To Prepare:

1. Cut two pieces of 8- by 10-inch rectangles of colorful fabric.

2. Putting the right sides together, machine stitch around three sides and half of the fourth side, giving a $\frac{1}{4}$-inch seam allowance. Turn the fabric right-side out.

☆ Activity:

1. Invite your child to make a little quilt with you. Say, "*q* is for *quilt.*" Have him say *q, quilt* several times.

2. Tell him to begin by stuffing craft stuffing or pulled cotton balls lightly into the prepared fabric. Hand stitch the opening closed.

3. Have him help you measure and cut fifteen pieces of yarn into 12-inch lengths.

4. Use chalk or washable marker to make dots on top of the quilt in a pattern of three rows across and five rows down. Explain that these are the places where he will quilt (stitch together) the fabric sandwich.

5. Thread the craft needle with yarn. Show him how to push the needle down on one side of a dot, then up on the other side, while leaving a tail above the quilt. Working together, cut the yarn, leaving a second tail of the same length. Tie a double knot to secure the yarn. Continue making stitches over the dots until the quilt is finished.

~ Q ~

QUART

Experimentation is a powerful way to learn things. Your child will remember her discoveries long after the lesson is finished when she finds the answers for herself.

☞ What You Need:
Paper, pencil, measuring cup, quart jar, water, black permanent marker

☆ Activity:
1. Write a big letter *q* on paper and show your child how to trace it with her fingers while saying its sound. Invite her to write more *q*'s of her own.

2. Now tell her that today she is learning what a quart is. Have her say *q, quart* several times.

3. Set out a measuring cup and a quart jar. Say the name of each item. Write a *q* on the jar with the black marker. Invite her to carefully fill the cup with water and pour it into the quart jar repeatedly until it is full. How many cups did it take to fill?

4. Ask her to empty the jar and repeat the process. Each time a cup of water is poured in, draw a black line on the side of the jar, along with the number of cups it represents.

5. Together, count up, "One, two, three, four. Four cups make a quart!"

Quart • 147

Q

Big Q, Little q Wall Hanging

You might like to refer to this pair as brothers and/or sisters named Q.

What You Need:
Paper, pencil, salt dough (see below), paper clips, cookie sheet, oven, poster paint, paintbrush, clear fixative

To Prepare:

Salt Dough
4 cups white flour
1 cup salt
$1\frac{1}{2}$ cups cold water

Stir together all ingredients. Put on a counter and knead until pliable. Add more flour or water to adjust consistency. Keep the dough covered and refrigerated when not in use.

Preheat the oven to 300 degrees before beginning the activity below.

Activity:
1. Invite your child to make a Big Q, Little q Wall Hanging. Explain that there are two ways to write the letter *q*. Write a small and a capital *q* on the paper. Point out that the capital (big) Q is made of a circle and a line. Ask him to trace the letters with his fingers and say their sound.

2. Demonstrate how to roll the salt dough into a snake shape. Invite him to make lots of snakes, then have him form them into a capital *Q* and a small *q*.

3. Fold open one side of two paper clips. Press them into the backs of the dough letters, leaving the loop extended at the top to form a hanger. If the letters are large, use two paper clips for each one to better support the weight.

4. Place the letters on a cookie sheet and bake at 300 degrees until light brown and completely dry. This may take an hour or more. Cool on a rack overnight.

5. Have him decorate the letters with several coats of poster paint, letting each layer dry before applying another. Spray with clear fixative and hang on a wall.

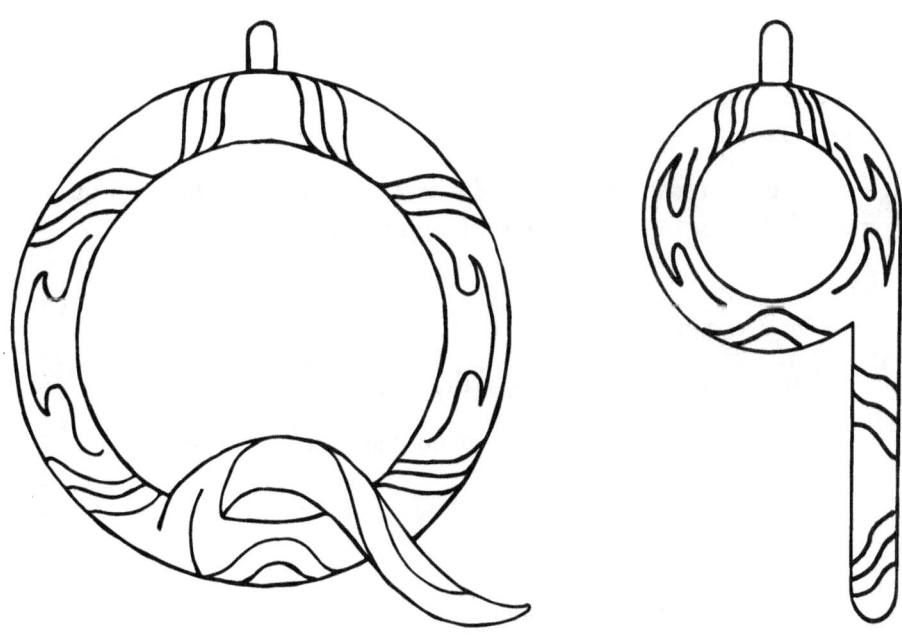

Q

Question Box

This lesson combines children's love of surprises with questions that exercise critical thinking skills.

☞ What You Need:
Lidded box, paper, pencil, scissors, colored markers

✂ To Prepare:
1. Decorate a lidded box with the letter *q* and question marks. This is the Question Box.
2. Cut paper into strips. Use colored markers to write one question on each piece. Fold the strips in half and place them in the box.

Examples:
- Can you name five colors?
- What kinds of animals live in the ocean?
- What could you make with a paper plate and crayons? Try it!
- What do you see in the night sky?
- Why should you brush your teeth?
- How tall are you? Let's find out!
- Where do bananas come from?
- If you had a pet lizard, what would you feed it?

☆ Activity:

1. Demonstrate, then invite your child to write a *q* on paper and say its sound. Now show her how to write a question mark (?). Explain that it means that a question is being asked.

2. Bring out the Question Box. Tell her that *q* is for *question* and have her repeat the phrase several times.

3. Invite her to open the box and take out one slip of paper. Ask her to point out the question mark. Read her the sentence, then ask her to respond as best she can. Help her research things she doesn't know the answers to.

4. Place the box in a convenient place and visit it once daily so she can choose a new strip. Make it a bit of a mystery; what will today's question be?

R

Rock People

Give your child's creativity free expression with this hands-on project.

☞ **What You Need:**
Smooth or interestingly shaped rocks, colored markers or poster paint, glue, paper, scissors, felt (optional)

☆ **Activity:**

1. Introduce the lesson by telling your child that today he is going to make Rock People. Say that *r* is the first sound in *rock*. Have him say *r, rock* a few times.

2. If you have previously collected the stones, set them out. Otherwise, ask him to search outside for smooth egg-sized rocks, then wash and dry them carefully.

3. Ask him to inspect the rocks, setting them on different sides and imagining what shapes they suggest. Urge him to try setting smaller ones, as heads, atop larger ones, which form the bodies. If he likes any of these arrangements, have him glue the pieces together and set them aside until dry.

4. As a final step, demonstrate how to draw on features with colored markers. Alternately, paint the figures and add features when dry. Glue on paper or felt hats, scarves, etc.

5. Encourage him to make a family of people, including pets. Display them on a plate or tray.

Rock People • 153

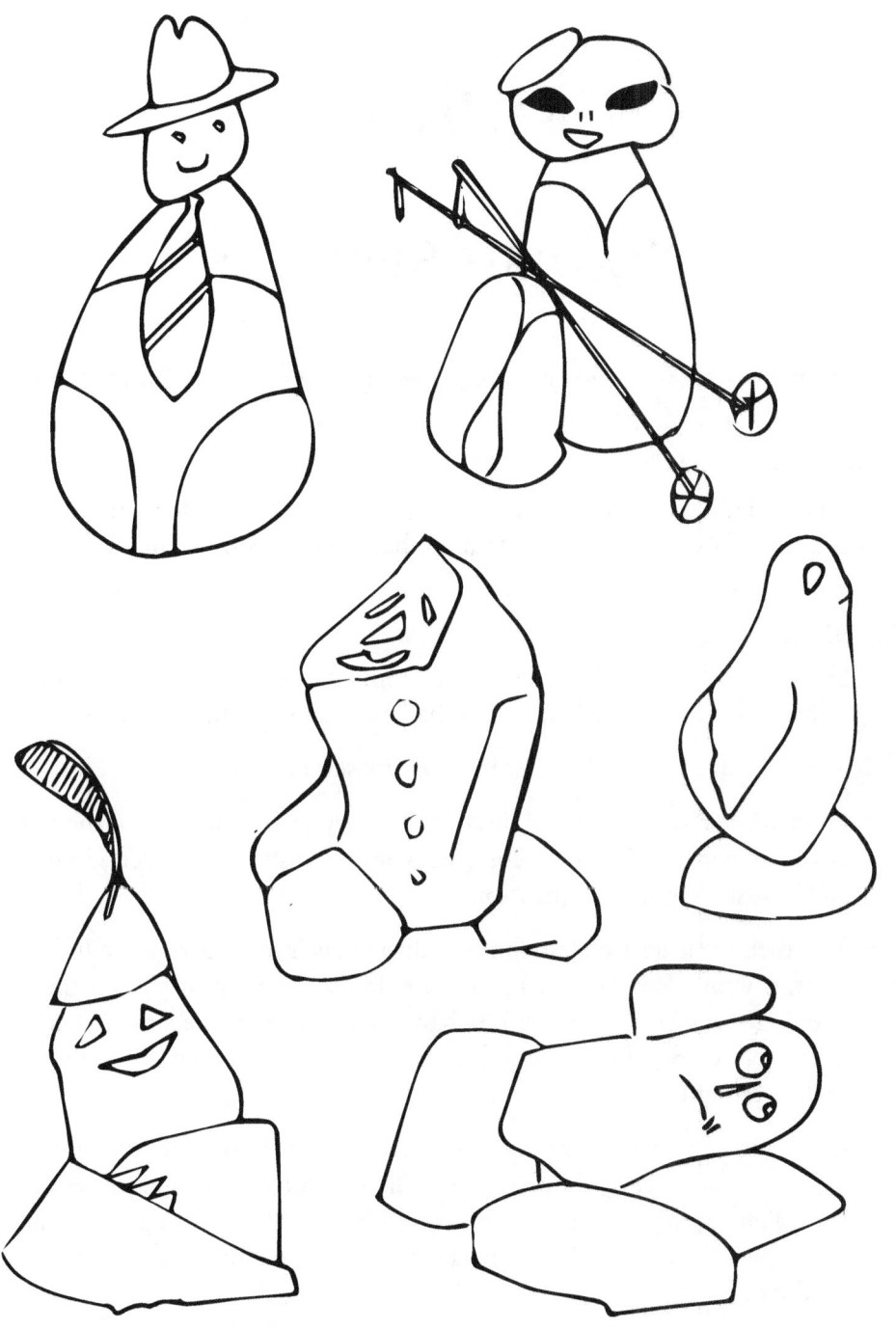

R

Radish Sprouts

Even if you don't have space for a garden, you can grow a bit of salad in your home.

☞ **What You Need:**
A radish, radish seeds for sprouting, measuring spoons, wide mouth quart jar, old nylon stocking or mesh, rubber band, black permanent marker

☆ **Activity:**

1. Show your child a radish. Together, examine it carefully and talk about how it looks, feels, and smells. Cut it in half and examine the inside. Taste it.

2. Say, "*r* is for *radish*." Have her say *r, radish* several times.

3. Look at the radish seeds and discuss how they grow when put in the right environment. Explain that people eat young radish plants called *sprouts* and that she is going to grow some.

4. Together, measure a tablespoon of radish seeds into a quart jar and fill it halfway with water. Stretch a piece of nylon stocking or mesh over the opening and secure with a rubber band. Write an *r* on the jar with the black marker. Set the jar away from direct sunlight and let the seeds soak overnight.

5. In the morning, have her drain the water. Tell her to rinse, drain, and inspect the seeds several times daily. When the first leaves appear, set the jar in light so the tiny plants can make chlorophyll and turn green. When the sprouts have nearly filled the jar, rinse them in a bowl of water to float off the hulls.

6. Invite her to taste the spicy greens. Include them in a salad or sandwich.

Radish Sprouts • 155

~ R ~

Rabbit Picture

After making this fluffy picture, invite your child to give the rabbit a name.

☞ What You Need:
Plain paper, construction paper, pencil, colored markers, cotton balls, pipe cleaners or yarn, glue, picture of a rabbit

☆ Activity:

1. Show your child a picture of a rabbit. Tell him that rabbits have long ears so they can hear very well, they have long back feet to help them hop, and they have large front teeth to gnaw with. Those teeth tell us that they are rodents, like mice, rats, and beavers. Explain that they like to eat grass and carrots, but they especially love tender garden greens.

2. Write the letter *r* on a sheet of plain paper and say its sound. Say, "*r* is for *rabbit.*" Ask him to say *r, rabbit,* then trace the letter with his fingers and write more of his own.

3. Draw an outline of a rabbit on a sheet of construction paper and have him write an *r* on the bottom corner.

4. Invite him to cover the rabbit with soft "fur" by gluing on bits of pulled-out cotton balls. Suggest he glue on pipe cleaners or yarn for whiskers.

5. Let the Rabbit Picture dry, then display. Encourage him to say *r* is for *rabbit* when showing it to friends.

R

Rice & Raisin Pudding

Top this tasty dish with sliced fruit and toasted nuts for a memorable dessert.

☞ What You Need:
Two plates, saucepan, pudding ingredients: rice, raisins, water, milk, sugar, salt, vanilla

☆ Activity:

1. Put some uncooked rice onto a plate. Ask your child to look at the seeds individually and swish her fingers through them. If you have different kinds of rice (short and long grain, white, brown, red, or basmati), set them out and have her compare them. Arrange the rice to form the letter *r*. Together say, "*r* is for *rice!*"

2. Set some raisins on the second plate. Explain that they are dried grapes. Have her examine them and eat some. Arrange the raisins to form an *r*. Together say, "*r* is for *raisins.*" Now point to the plates in turn and say, "*r* is for *rice* and *r* is for *raisins!*"

3. Make a batch of rice pudding, letting her help measure and stir the ingredients.

4. When the dessert is served, encourage her to herald its arrival by announcing the following: *r* is for *rice* and *raisin pudding!*

Rice & Raisin Pudding
Delicious served warm or chilled.

Step 1
Mix the following ingredients in a saucepan. Bring to a boil, then cover and simmer over low heat, stirring occasionally, until the water is nearly absorbed, approximately 15 to 20 minutes.
1 cup medium-grain rice
2 cups water
1/4 teaspoon salt

Step 2
Slowly stir in:
3 cups whole milk
1 1/2 cups half-and-half
2/3 cup sugar (or less, if desired)

Simmer uncovered 30–40 minutes until thick. Stir often to keep it from sticking or burning. Toward the end of this process stir in:
1/2 – 3/4 cup raisins

Step 3
Remove from heat and stir in:
1 teaspoon vanilla extract

~ S ~

SALT PAPERWEIGHT

Young children can use this project to make a beautiful gift. Older children and adults enjoy the challenge of forming intricate designs.

☞ What You Need:

Small jars with lids (such as baby food jars), food color, salt, several small bowls, plates, pie pan, funnel (optional)

✂ To Prepare:

1. Decide how many colors you will use. For each color, put ½ to 1 cup salt in a bowl.

2. Add drops of food color and mix vigorously with a fork to blend.

3. Pour the colored salt onto plates and let dry overnight.

☆ Activity:

1. Invite your child to look at and touch the different colors of salt. Say, "*s* is for *salt*." Have him say *s, salt* several times. Pour some colored salt in a pie pan and show him how to trace the letter *s* in it with his fingers.

2. Demonstrate, then invite him to spoon layers of colored salt into a jar, gently tapping the sides to settle it as he works. Use a funnel to direct the flow, if desired.

3. Cap the bottle when it is completely full. If it settles after a day, add enough salt to top it off.

Salt Paperweight • 161

~ S ~

SNOWMAN NOTECARD

Holiday notecards are fun to make and give. Try this version to keep little hands busy.

☞ What You Need:

Construction paper, pencil, scissors, glue, decorating items (colored markers, sequins, glitter, fabric and felt scraps, cotton balls, etc.)

Note: Supervise your child closely if she uses sequins or glitter so she doesn't ingest them.

☆ Activity:

1. Invite your child to make a Snowman Card. Together, fold a sheet of colored construction paper in half.

2. Say, *"s is for snowman."* Have her say *s, snowman* several times. Write a large *s* on the inside front panel of the card. Ask her to trace over it, first with her fingers, then with a pencil, each time saying its sound.

3. Discuss what body parts and features her snowman will have. Cut two circles from white construction paper and have her glue them on the face of the card.

4. Invite her to add features and accessories with colored markers or by attaching bits of paper, fabric, lace, or sequins. To make a fluffy snowman, glue on clumps pulled from cotton balls.

5. Ask her who she would like to give the notecard to and what short message she wants to include. Write it in the card and have her give or send it to the friend.

Snowman Card • 163

S

Soap Bubbles

Your child will be delighted when his efforts produce a bowlful of bubbles!

☞ **What You Need:**
Bar of plain soap such as Ivory, grater, bowl, warm water, hand-powered egg beater, food color (optional)

☆ **Activity:**

1. Set out the materials and explain to your child that he is going to grate the soap into the bowl, then pour in warm water and beat it to make lots of bubbles.

2. Tell him that *soap* begins with the letter *s*. Write the letter on paper, then have him practice writing it and saying its sound a few times.

3. Explain that soap is made using natural fats and oils from plants and animals. If you have different varieties, compare them.

4. Demonstrate how to the use the grater safely, then invite him to grate the soap into the bowl. (Be sure to supervise closely so he doesn't cut himself.)

5. Add warm water and encourage him to beat the mixture with the old fashioned egg beater until he has a bowlful of suds. Add food coloring, if desired.

Note: If using a hand beater is too difficult, together, whip the soap with an electric mixer.

Soap Bubbles · 165

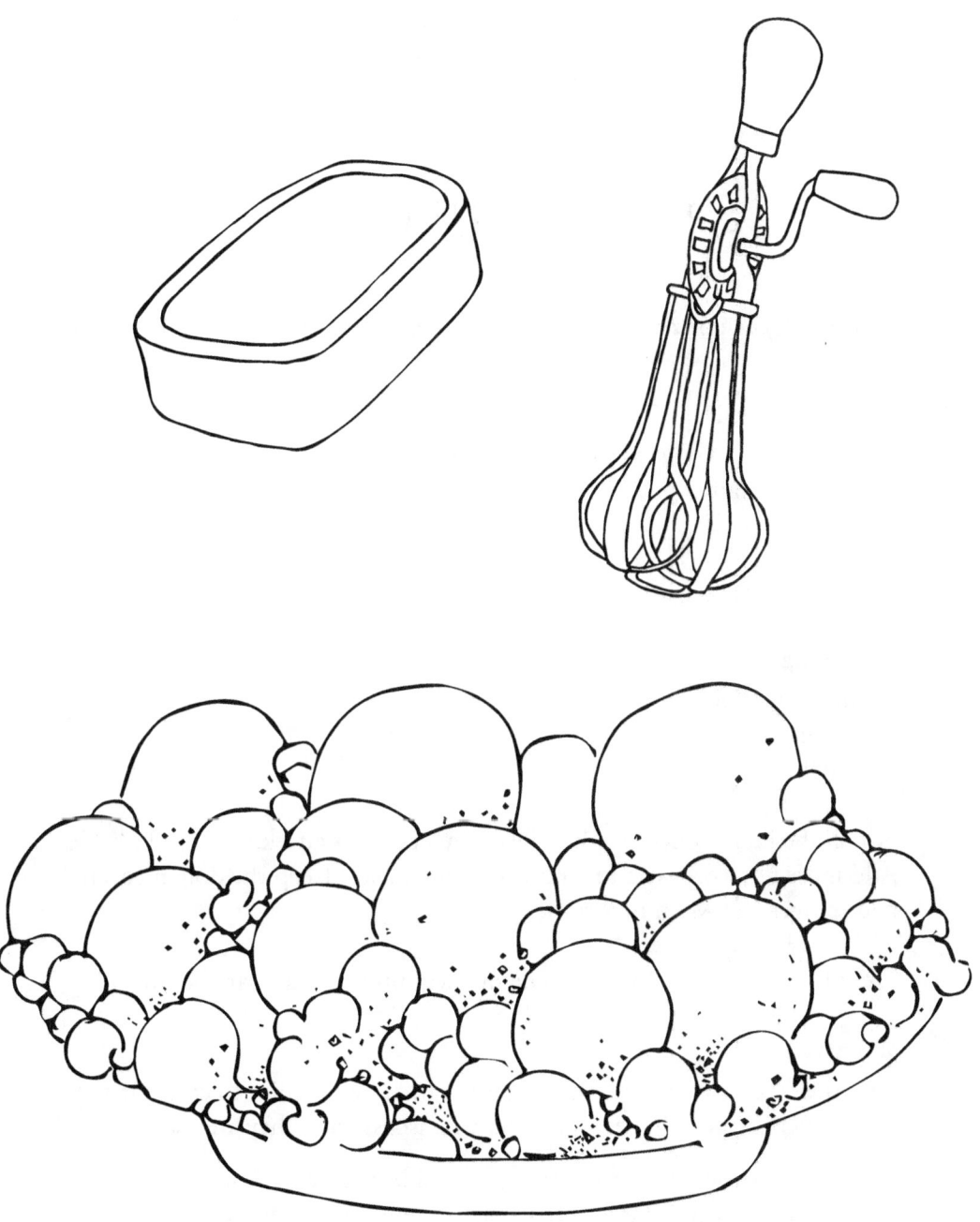

S

Spoon Sculptures

Brightly colored spoons make a nice addition to kitchen decor.

☞ What You Need:
Assorted sized spoons, salt dough, pencil, paper, oven, cookie sheet, poster paint, clear fixative

✂ To Prepare:

Salt Dough
4 cups white flour
1 cup salt
$1\frac{1}{2}$ cups cold water

Stir all the ingredients together. Place on a counter and knead until pliable. Add more flour or water to adjust the consistency. Keep the dough covered and refrigerated when not in use.

Preheat the oven to 300 degrees before beginning the activity below.

☆ Activity:
1. Set out several spoons of different sizes. Invite your child to examine them and describe their shapes and patterns. Discuss what they are used for.

2. Demonstrate how to arrange the spoons side by side in order from smallest to largest. Now mix them and ask her to repeat the exercise.

3. Say, "*s* is for *spoon.*" Write a large *s* on paper, then have her trace the letter with her fingers and again with pencil while saying its sound.

4. Let her play freely with the salt dough for a time. Demonstrate, then have her make spoon shapes herself. Press a pencil through the end of each handle to make a hole for hanging.

5. Place the pieces on a cookie sheet and bake at 300 degrees until light brown and completely dry. This may take an hour or more, depending on thickness. Cool on a rack overnight to allow any remaining moisture to dissipate.

6. Invite her to decorate her Spoon Sculptures with several layers of poster paint, letting the pieces dry between each coat. Spray with clear fixative and hang on a wall.

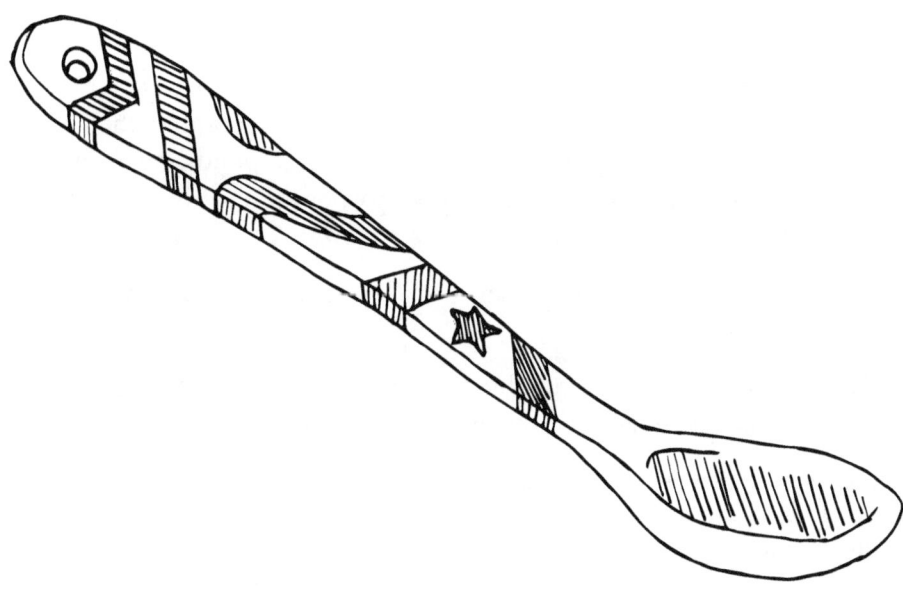

~ T ~

Walnut Shell Turtles

Introduce the letter t *while learning about these peculiar animals. Then make a group of these cute little turtles.*

☞ **What You Need:**
Pictures of turtles, halved walnut shells, construction paper, scissors, glue

☆ **Activity:**

1. Look at pictures of turtles with your child. Explain that they are reptiles like snakes and lizards, but unlike those creatures they protect their bodies in shells. Turtles spend part or most of their time in ponds, rivers, or oceans. Tortoises live on land. The upper part of the shell is called the *carapace,* while the lower part is called a *plastron.*

2. Say, "*t* is for *turtle.*" Have him say *t, turtle* several times and practice writing the letter.

3. Demonstrate how to cut and glue four little paper feet, a tail, and a head onto a walnut shell half, then invite him to make more of his own.

4. Display the turtles on a desk or table. Alternately, set several in a box lined with sand or moss, with a tiny artificial pond built from a bit of foil filled with water.

Walnut Shell Turtles • 169

T

Tea Party

How many things can your child find that start with the letter t? *This activity challenges her to test names herself to find which items to include in her party.*

☞ **What You Need:**
Paper, scissors, colored markers, items that begin with the letter *t* (tea, teapot, teacup, tray, toast, tablecloth, towel, teaspoon, tablespoon, table, teddy bear)

✂ **To Prepare:**
Cut a sheet of paper into twelve pieces.

☆ **Activity:**

1. Invite your child to share a *t* tea party with you. Begin by showing her how to write the letter *t* on paper and say its sound. Encourage her to practice this a few times.

2. Ask her to write with colored marker a *t* on each piece of prepared paper.

3. Urge her to find and gather lots of things that begin with *t*.

4. Together, prepare a table for the tea party, using as many *t* items as possible. Include an extra chair or place for a favorite *teddy bear*.

5. Make some toast and brew the tea. While it is steeping, talk about the many *t* things at the table (including where the tea and toast will go . . . in your *tummy!*) Have her place a *t* paper near each object that begins with that letter, reminding her to say its sound and the item's name each time.

6. Serve the tea and enjoy the *t* tea party!

Tea Party • 171

T

Tent

Who says you need fancy toys to have fun? Just provide a cozy space and possibly a friend . . . and let the adventures begin!

☞ **What You Need:**
Broomstick or wooden dowel, two chairs, blanket or sheet, paper, colored markers, safety pin

☆ **Activity:**
1. Rest the broomstick or dowel on the backs of two chairs. Make a tent by draping the blanket or sheet over it.
2. With your child watching, write a large letter *t* on a sheet of paper. Invite him to trace it and say its sound.
3. Say, "*t* is for *tent.*" Have him say *t, tent* several times. Attach the *t* paper to the side of the tent with a safety pin.
4. Invite him to sit in the tent with you or a friend. Together, think of more words that begin with *t,* then take turns telling stories using those words.

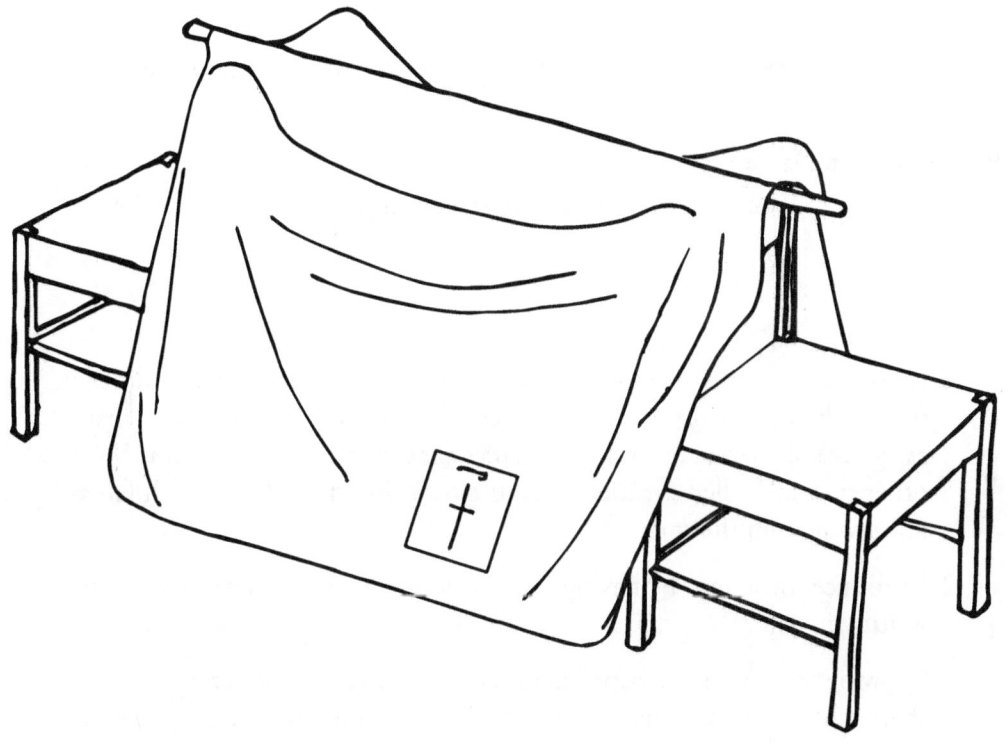

T

TREE

Trees are all around us. Help your child take a closer look with this art project.

What You Need:
Real trees and/or pictures of trees, construction paper, scissors, cardboard toilet roll

Activity:

1. Look at different species of trees with your child. Note how they differ in overall shape. Discuss variations in leaf shapes and bark. Point out that *evergreens* like pine and fir have needles that they keep year round. Most other trees are called *deciduous* because they drop their leaves each fall and regrow them in the spring.

2. Introduce the letter *t* by having her say *t* is for *tree* a few times and practice writing it.

3. Show her how to make paper trees. For each one, cut two green tree shapes, as shown. Cut halfway down the centerline from the top of one tree. Cut halfway up the centerline from the bottom of the second tree. Slide the two cut pieces together and attach to a paper base cut from a cardboard toilet roll (or construction paper), as shown. Help her make as many trees as she likes, then place them on a table to form a little forest.

Tree · 175

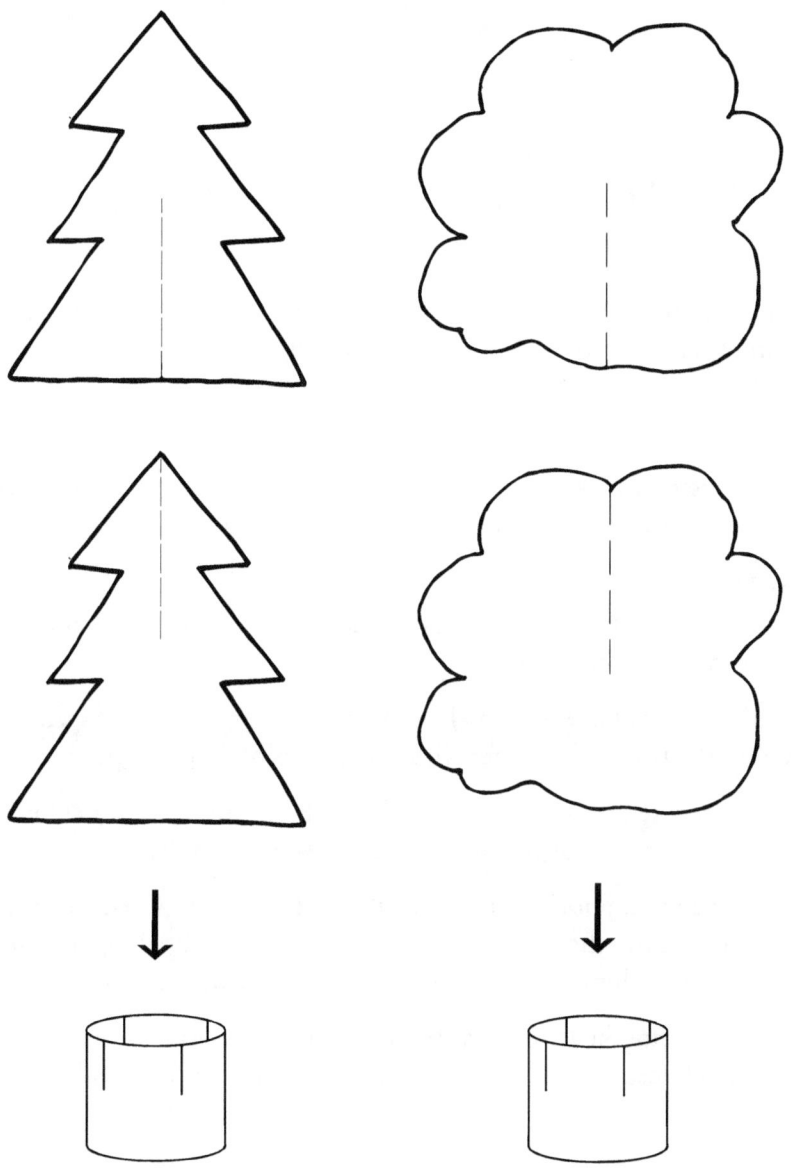

U

Umbrella Watercolor

Rainy days are perfect for this activity! Encourage your child decorate his art with whatever supplies are handy and let his creativity surprise you.

☞ **What You Need:**
Paper, watercolor paper, construction paper, pencil, scissors, tape, watercolor paints, jar of water, large watercolor paintbrush, tray

☆ **Activity:**

1. Say, "*u* is for umbrella." Have your child say *u, umbrella* several times and practice writing the letter.

2. Together, cut out a few umbrella shapes from construction paper. Attach them to the watercolor paper with tiny pieces of looped tape.

3. Set the prepared paper on the tray, then ask him to brush watercolor paint over the entire page using broad strokes. Set aside to dry.

4. Suggest he make another picture while the first dries. When a page is dry, have him remove the umbrella shapes to reveal the unpainted designs beneath. Invite him to decorate the umbrellas further, if desired.

5. Have him write the letter *u* in the corner of his favorite piece and then help you choose a place to hang the picture where it can be admired.

Umbrella Watercolor • 177

꙰ U ꙰

Under and Up!

Similar to familiar sink and float experiments, this activity highlights the letter u while guiding your child to make a series of tests and then record her observations.

☞ What You Need:
Paper, construction paper, pencil, stickers, bowl of water, collection of small items (a cork, feather, small piece of sponge, paper clip, cereal, rubber band, small wad of paper and foil, etc.)

✂ To Prepare:
Draw a chart on construction paper, as shown.

☆ Activity:
1. Introduce the lesson by writing the letter *u* on a piece of paper and saying its sound. Tell your child that *u* is for *under*. Ask her to show you what that means by, for example, crawling under a table. Now say that *u* is also for *up*. She might express this by jumping up or standing on a chair. Have her say *u* is for *under* and *u* is for *up*.

2. Bring out the bowl of water and explain that she is going to test various things to see whether they stay under the water or go up.

3. Ask her to collect a few small items. Have her choose one object, guess the result, then test her hypothesis by pushing it under the water to the bottom of the bowl before releasing it. Does it stay *under* or go *up*?

4. Bring out the prepared chart and review it with her. Add the name of each item as she tests it, then have her add a sticker in the correct place.

	under	up
dime	🍎	
leaf		🍎
cork		🍎
paperclip	🍎	
raw egg		
hard-boiled egg		

U

Rainy Day Umbrellas

What does a rainy day make you think of? Why umbrellas, of course! What else comes to mind while walking in the rain? Capture those impressions with this fanciful display.

☞ **What You Need:**
   Construction paper, scissors, tape or glue, colored markers

☆ **Activity:**

1. Cut a set of large fanciful paper umbrellas with your child. Invite him to decorate them as much as he likes. Demonstrate, then have him write the letter *u* on some of them, saying *u* is for *umbrella* each time.

2. Invite him to glue or tape the umbrellas onto a bulletin board, sheet of poster board, or wall.

3. Together, cut blue construction paper raindrops and add them artfully among the umbrellas.

4. Discuss what he might find or see on a rainy day. Suggest he add people in rain gear or a few animals to the picture.

Rainy Day Umbrellas

U

U Is for Underwear

An important part of growing up is learning how to organize one's things. By giving your child the opportunity to choose how to arrange all her stuff, you include her in the decision making process. This helps her feel empowered as she controls her environment, in contrast to just following rules imposed by others.

☞ **What You Need:**
Paper, colored pencils, underwear

☆ **Activity:**

1. Invite your child to watch you write the letter *u*. Say its sound. Have her write the letter with different colored pencils, saying its sound each time.

2. Say, "*u* is for *underwear.*" Have her say *u, underwear* several times. Ask her to name types of underwear she has.

3. Together, go to her underwear drawer. Ask her to dump the contents onto her bed and set aside items that no longer fit or she never wears. (Donate, discard, or repurpose the clothing as you wish.)

4. Next, have her sort the remaining pieces into piles of like items. Show her how to match the socks and fold (or roll) the clothing.

5. Invite her to arrange the underwear drawer herself, following a pattern that she finds pleasing.

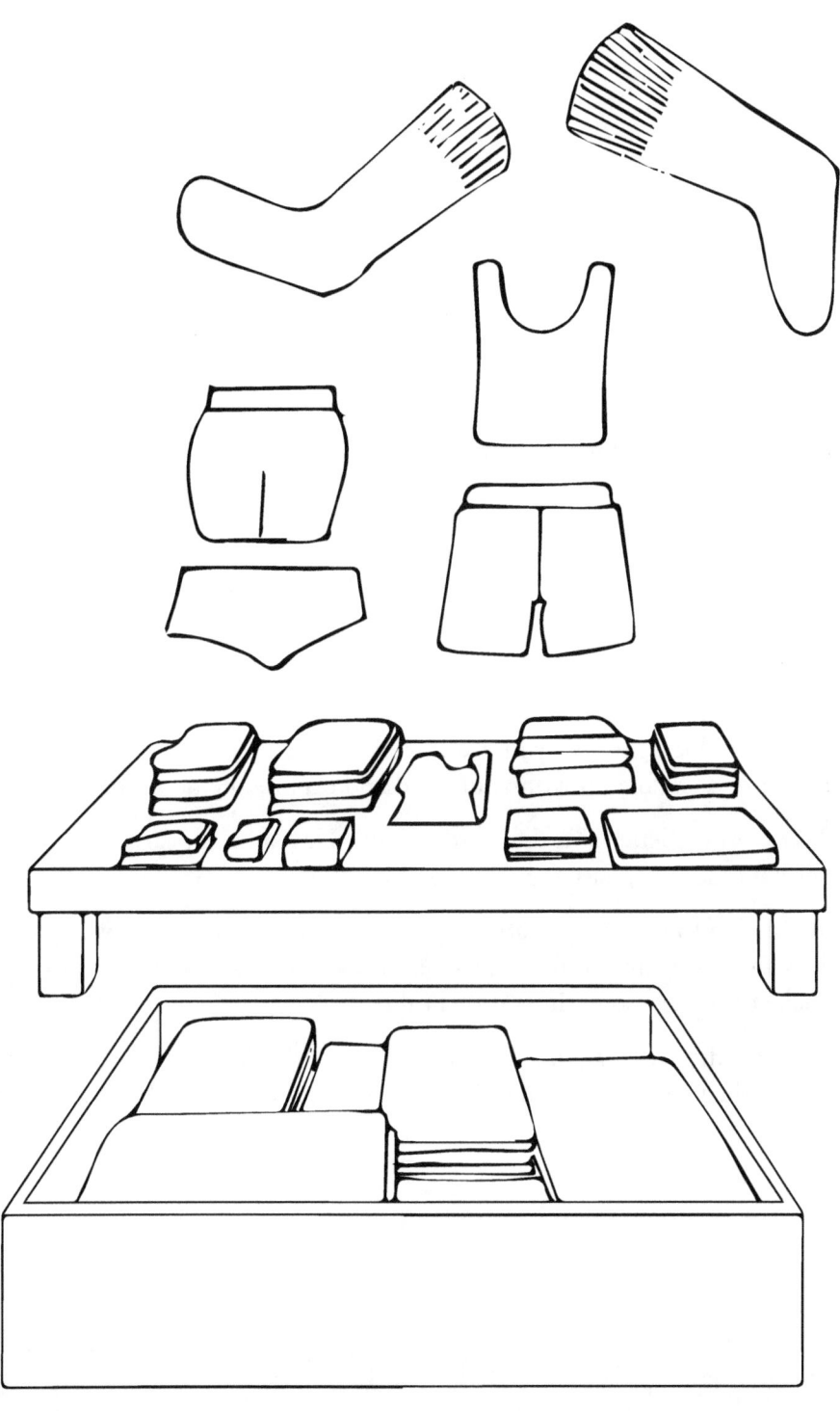

V

VOLCANO

Here are directions for making a simple "volcano." If you are interested in doing more complex projects, search online for other options.

☞ What You Need:
Book on volcanoes, play dough or clay, vinegar, baking soda, measuring spoons

☆ Activity:

1. Visit your local library's youth department and check out a book on volcanoes. Cuddle up with your child and explore the book together.

2. Point out the letter *v* in the word *volcano*. Have him repeat the word several times, emphasizing the *v* sound.

3. Invite him to build a miniature volcano with playdough or clay. Suggest he scratch a *v* into the side. Have him press a bowl shape into the top to make the crater (sometimes called caldera).

4. Now for the exciting part. Ask him to put two tablespoons vinegar in the crater, then add a teaspoon of baking soda and watch it bubble and froth!

Volcano

❧ V ❧

Vanilla Milkshake

What a tasty introduction to the letter v!

☞ **What You Need:**
Pictures of vanilla beans, paper, colored pencils, tape, drinking glass, vanilla yogurt or ice cream, vanilla extract, milk, blender, violin music (optional)

☆ **Activity:**
1. Open a bottle of vanilla extract and invite your child to smell it. Explain that it is made by soaking vanilla beans in alcohol and water. Look at pictures of the tropical vines, noting their pretty flowers and the long thin pods that grow from them. Discuss foods that have vanilla flavors: yogurt, ice cream, cookies, cakes, candies, puddings, and drinks. Taste any vanilla flavored foods you have.

2. Note the word *vanilla* on the packaging of the food you tasted, paying special attention to the letter *v*. Have her say *v, vanilla* a few times. Demonstrate, then ask her to write some *v*'s with colored pencils.

3. Now have her write her best *v* on a slip of paper and tape it to the drinking glass.

4. Letting her help as she is able, place a few scoops of vanilla yogurt or ice cream in a blender. Add a tiny splash of vanilla extract and enough milk to cover. Blend until smooth.

5. Pour the milkshake into the *v* glass. Enjoy the drink while listening to *violin* music.

V

Vegetable Salad

Here's another opportunity for your child to make decisions for himself. In this case, about the choice and arrangement of ingredients.

☞ **What You Need:**
Lettuce and assorted salad vegetables and toppings, knife, salad bowls, tray, salad dressing (optional)

☆ **Activity:**

1. Announce to your child that today he gets to help you make a vegetable salad. Have him say *v* is for *vegetable* with you a few times and show him how to trace the shape with his fingers on a tabletop. Explain that the base of the salad will be lettuce, but he can choose the toppings. Discuss what other vegetables (carrots, cucumbers, tomatoes, radishes, bell peppers, avocados, beets, etc.) he would like to include. Ask what else he would like on his salad: hard-cooked egg, cottage cheese, kidney beans, garbanzo beans, canned corn, cheese cubes, olives, etc.

2. Begin by having him wash his hands and then tear lettuce leaves into individual salad bowls. Next, cut the chosen vegetables into bite-size pieces and set them in individual piles on the tray, letting him help as he is able.

3. Invite him to arrange the cut vegetables and assorted toppings over the lettuce. Suggest he make a *v* on the salads with some ingredient.

4. Congratulate him on his creation. Add a bit of salad dressing, if desired, and enjoy a meal together.

Vegetable Salad · 189

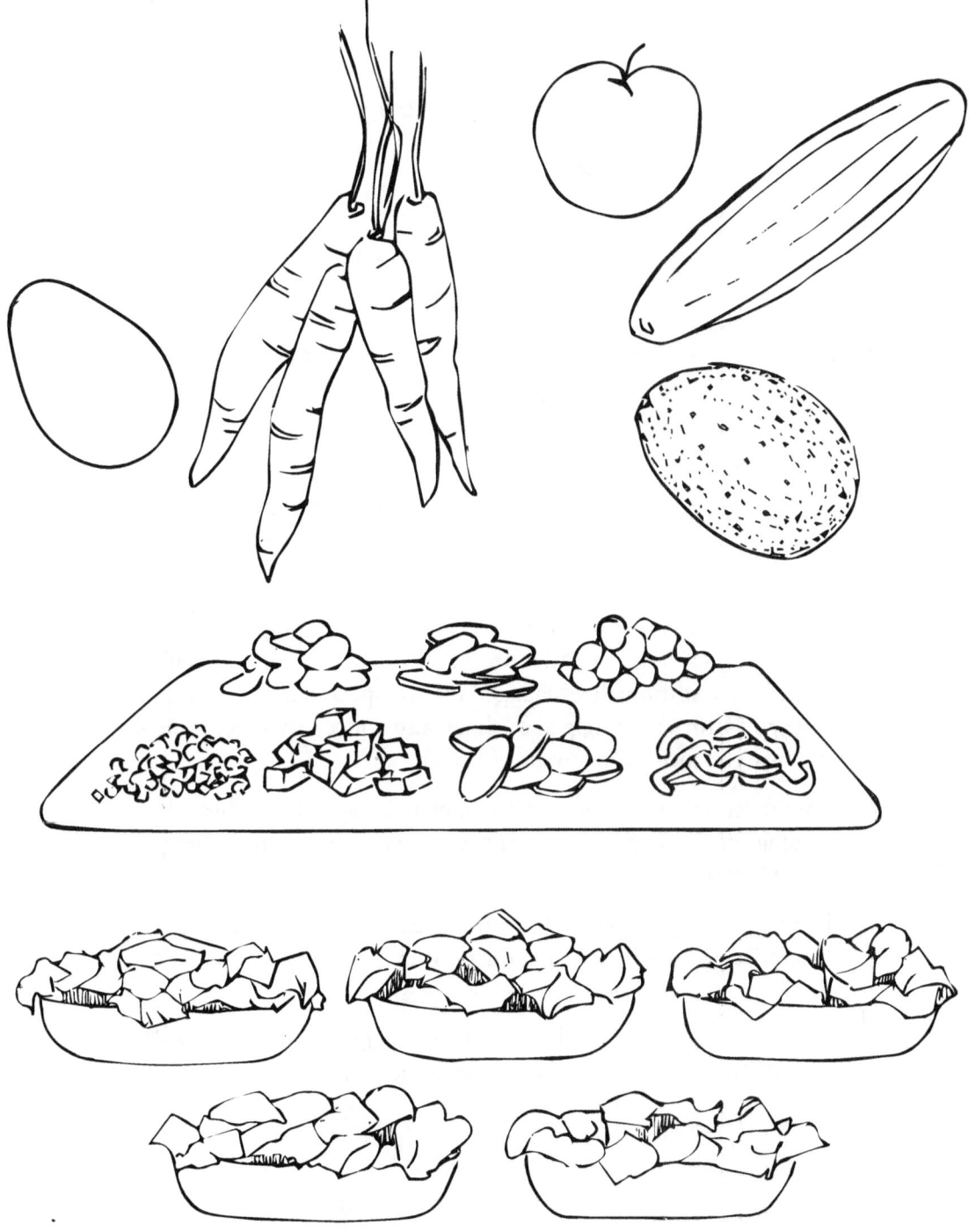

❦ V ❧

VALENTINE

This project gives your child a way to express her love and gratitude to family members and friends. Ask her to think about why she cares for each person as she makes their card.

☞ What You Need:
Construction paper, scissors, glue, flower pictures, crayons

☆ Activity:

1. Tell your child that *v* is for *valentine* and have her repeat the phrase several times. Explain that Valentine's Day cards mean "I love you" and that they are traditionally exchanged on one special day each year (February 14th). Heart shaped cards are also a nice way to let someone know that you love them any time of year.

2. Write the letter *v*, then demonstrate how to make it into a heart by extending the lines up and over to complete the shape. Invite her to draw lots of *v* hearts of her own.

3. When she is ready, show her how to make a valentine by cutting a construction paper heart, gluing on a flower picture, then decorating it with lots of crayon hearts.

4. Suggest she make cards for those she loves. Help her address envelopes and mail the valentines or deliver them in person.

❧ W ❧

W Is for Wood

Simple wooden blocks are used to introduce the letter w *in this lesson. Wooden beads, chopsticks, or other items can be substituted if you don't have blocks.*

☞ **What You Need:**
Wooden blocks (or other movable items made of wood), paper, pencil

☆ **Activity:**
1. Say, "*w* is for *wood.*" Have your child say *w, wood* several times. Discuss the fact that wood comes from trees.

2. Ask him to walk around your home and point out items that are made of wood. Then have him bring out his wooden blocks.

3. Write the letter *w* on paper. Have him trace it with his fingers, say its sound, and then print more of them.

4. Together, build a large *w* with the blocks. Ask him to trace the shape with his hand, then suggest he add other wooden toys and play freely for awhile.

W Is for Wood • 193

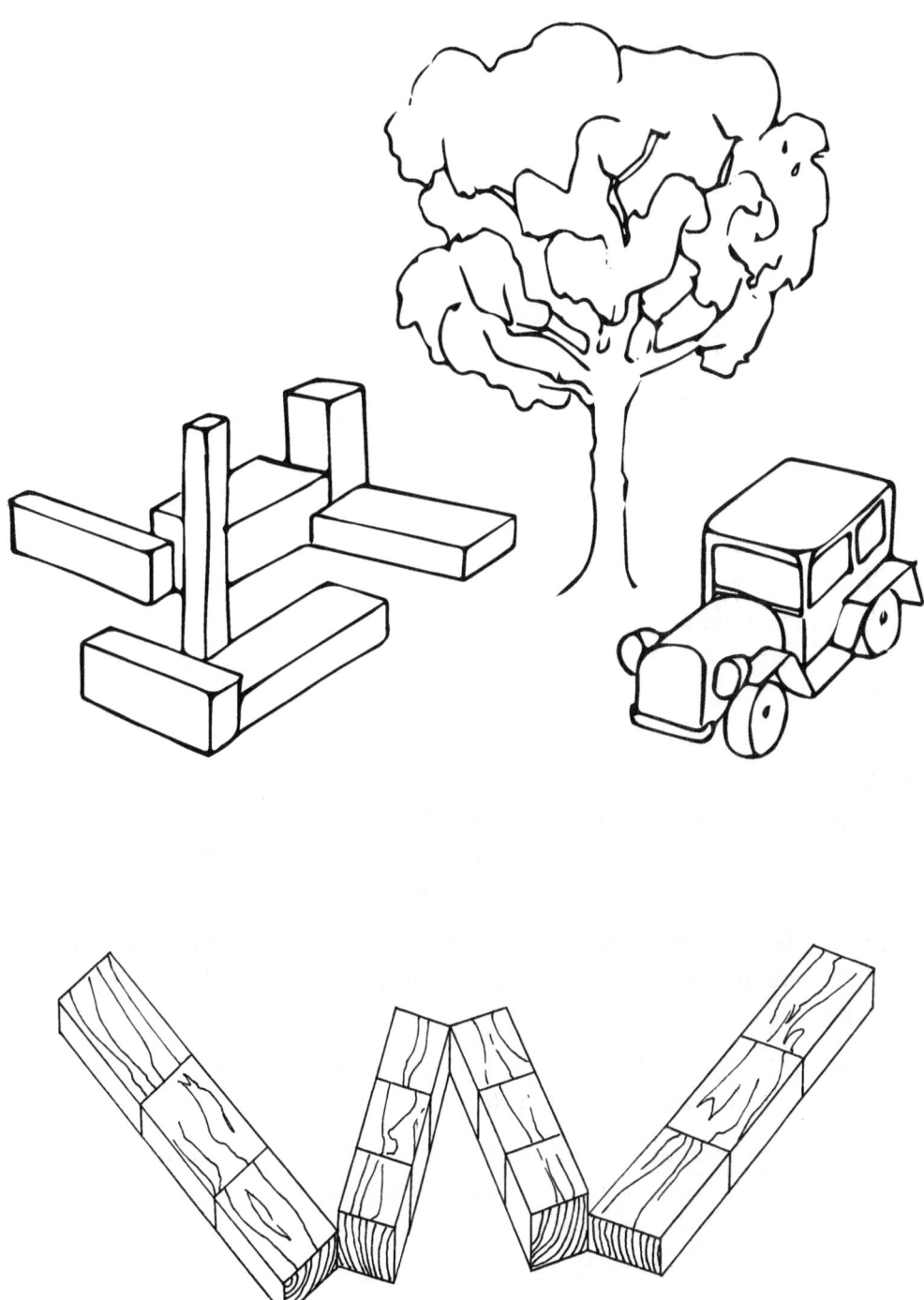

W

Walnut Balls

Watch your child smile with pride when she serves this dessert that she made herself!

Note: If your child is allergic to walnuts, skip this activity.

☞ What You Need:
Pictures of walnut trees, whole walnuts (both shelled and unshelled, if possible), nutcracker, dates, butter, salt, vanilla, shredded coconut, food processor, bowl, plate

☆ Activity:
1. Set out an unshelled walnut. Explain that *w* is the first sound in *walnut*. Have her practice saying *w, walnuts* several times. Crack open the nut. Together, inspect the interior, then smell and taste it.

2. Show her pictures of the huge trees walnuts grow on. Note the leathery covering (husk) that encloses the hard nut, which is actually a walnut tree seed.

3. Set out a pile of shelled walnuts. Form a *w* with them, then scramble the pieces and ask her to reform the letter.

4. Explain that walnuts are a very nutritious food and that you are going to make a snack with them. Invite her to help measure the ingredients.

Walnut Balls

Put the following ingredients into a food processor and blend until you have a crunchy paste:

1 cup walnuts, raw or toasted
½ cup dates, pitted
2 tablespoons butter
½ teaspoon vanilla
⅛ teaspoon salt

Scoop the mixture into a bowl. Working together, form small portions into balls, then roll them in shredded coconut and set them on the plate. (If the paste is too sticky to work with, chill it in the refrigerator for a bit to firm it up.) Store the snacks in the refrigerator or freezer.

Suggest she arrange her creation on a pretty plate and serve it for dessert. Have her practice writing *w*'s, then print her best one on a card and set it by the plate. Encourage her to introduce her dish as *w, Walnut Balls!*

W

W Is for Water

Water is remarkable in its many forms. This lesson is a great introduction to its unique properties.

☞ **What You Need:**
Paper, pencil, poster board or construction paper, glue, water, ice cube, pan of boiling water, assorted small containers, large bowl, baster, food color (optional); pictures of water, ice, and steam

☆ **Activity:**

1. Explain to your child that today he is going to play with water. Write a large letter *w* on a piece of paper. Have him say *w* is for *water* with you a few times. Invite him to trace the *w* with his fingers and then practice writing it with a pencil.

2. Set out assorted containers and a large bowl. Encourage him to play with water by pouring it from container to container over the bowl. For more fun, add a bit of food color or suggest he squirt it from a baster.

3. Bring a pot of water to boil and invite him to watch the steam. Catch some of the water vapor on a plate or pan lid and observe it return to liquid. Taste it. Next, look at an ice cube and watch it melt. Discuss the three states of water: solid, liquid, and gas.

4. Together, look at and discuss pictures of ice, water, and steam (or draw pictures of your own). Write a *w* at the top of a sheet of poster board or construction paper (glue several sheets together, if desired). Invite him to arrange and glue the pictures onto the display.

Picture Ideas

- Liquid: glass of water, rain, ocean, river, lake

- Frozen: ice cubes, iceberg, glacier, hail, snow, snow cone, ice skating rink or frozen pond

- Gas: geyser, steaming teapot, fog, mist, steaming cup of coffee, steaming pie or plate of food

W

Wood Wall Hanging

Construct a one-of-a-kind art piece using the resources around you. If you don't have access to nature, collect whatever is in your environment and make the wall hanging from that. The important point is that the base is made of wood.

☞ **What You Need:**
Branch or driftwood, sandpaper (optional), string or yarn, scissors, glue, small items collected on a nature walk (feathers, dried grass, pinecones, rocks, flowers, shells, etc.)

☆ **Activity:**

1. Invite your child to walk with you and find a branch or piece of driftwood, along with small items from nature to decorate it. Remind her that *w* is for *wood* and have her repeat the phrase. Have her scratch the letter into dirt or sand with a stick.

2. Once a branch is selected, instruct her to wash and dry it, then sand it, if desired.

3. Later, suggest she arrange the items on and beneath the branch in different ways until she finds a pleasing pattern.

4. Help her to complete the project by gluing some pieces onto the branch and tying on other to hang from it.

5. Tie a string to each end of the Wood Wall Hanging and display it on a wall or from a ceiling hook.

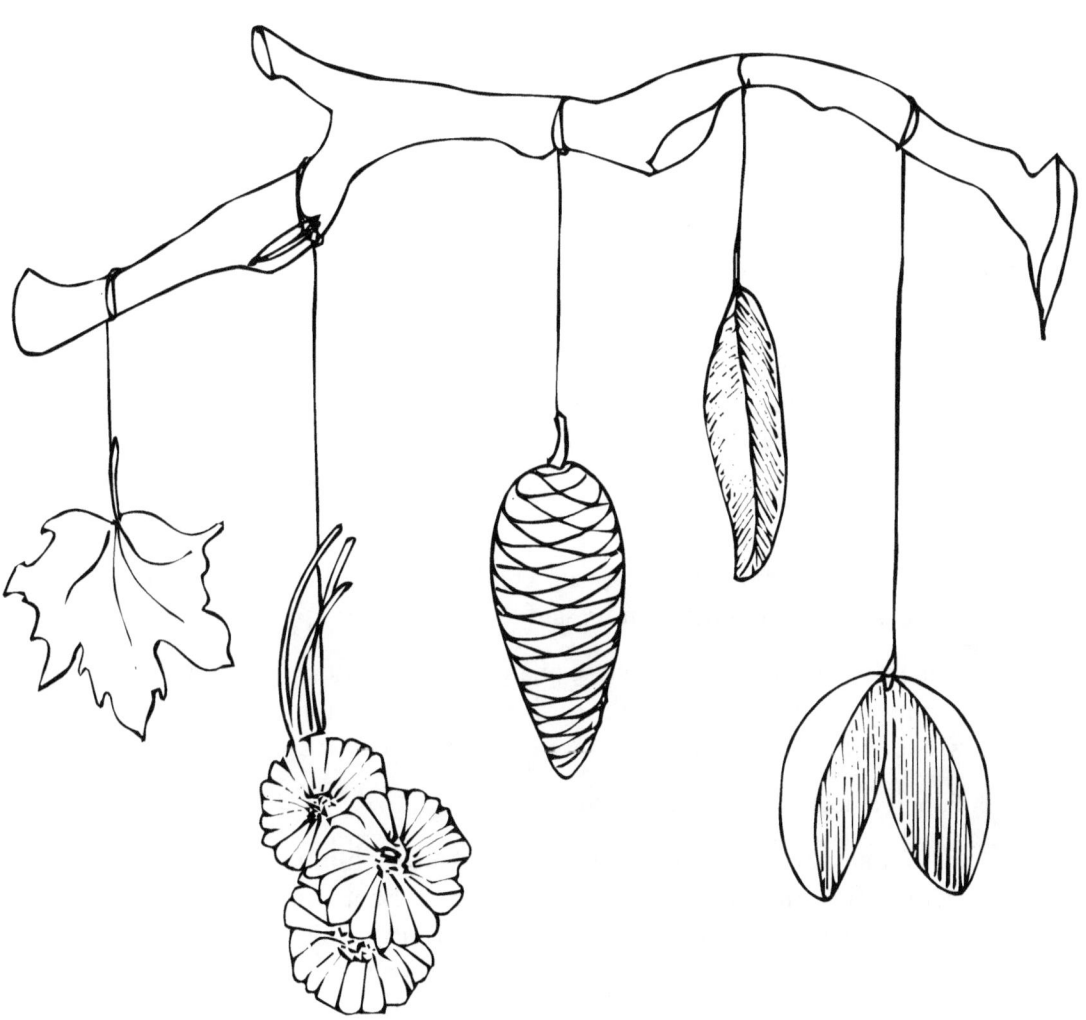

⚡ X ⚡

X Necklace

This project is a delightful introduction to the letter x. *Make sure to choose child friendly items as decorations.*

☞ **What You Need:**
Paper, pencil, cardstock, scissors, yarn or ribbon, hole punch, glue, decorative items (colored cereal pieces, pasta, candies, etc.)

☆ **Activity:**
1. Introduce the lesson by telling your child that the sound of *x* is actually made up of two sounds, *k* and *s,* said together as *ks*.

2. Cut an *x* shape from cardstock. Explain that *x* is written by making two downward slant lines. Trace the cardstock *x* with your fingers as you would write it. Say its sound. Have him repeat your actions.

3. Punch a hole in the top two arms of the *x*.

4. Set out an assortment of decorative items and ask him to point out his favorite. Tell him to glue those onto the left-to-right slant line, which is the first line made when forming the letter. (Putting his favorite trimmings along this line helps him remember to "go this way first.")

5. Have him choose a second kind of decoration (with a different shape or color) and glue those pieces along the right-to-left slant line. Set the project aside to dry.

6. String yarn or a ribbon through the holes. Invite him to wear his *x* necklace and show it to others.

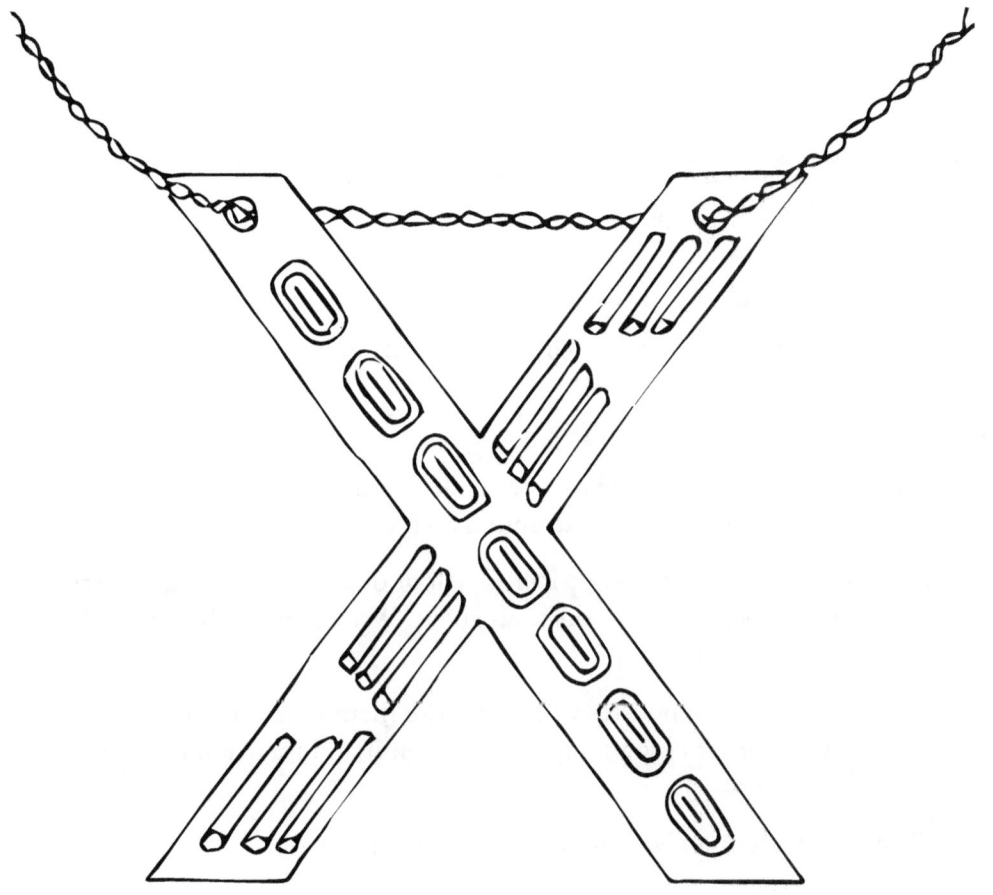

℘ X ℘

X Card

A handmade card, delivered by post or in person, is a rarity these days. Receiving one will brighten a loved one's day.

☞ **What You Need:**
Paper, construction paper, pencil, crayons or colored markers, stickers

☆ **Activity:**

1. Write a large *x* on paper. Have your child to trace it with her fingers, then write more *x*'s herself, saying its sound each time.

2. Fold a sheet of construction paper in half or quarters to make a notecard. Ask her to choose a person she cares about. Write down a short note that she dictates for that person.

3. Explain that *x*'s mean kisses when we write them in letters. Invite her to decorate the card by writing lots of *x*'s on it and then adding some colorful stickers.

4. Have her mail or deliver the card to the special person.

X

X Bookmark

The next time you stop reading a bedtime story partway through a book, use one of these handy bookmarks and mention that "x marks the spot!"

☞ What You Need:
Cardstock, construction paper, clear contact paper, ruler, scissors, glue, colored markers,

✄ To Prepare:
1. For each bookmark, cut a $1\frac{1}{2}$-inch by 8-inch piece of cardstock.
2. Cut thin strips of colored construction paper and set aside. Your child will use them to make *x*'s on the bookmark.

☆ Activity:
1. Introduce the activity by reviewing the sound and shape of *x* with your child. Emphasize that when writing, the first slanted line is drawn from top left to bottom right.
2. Invite him to decorate a prepared cardstock bookmark by gluing on crosses made from the paper strips. Encourage him to say the *x* sound each time he glues on a letter.
3. When the project is dry, suggest he add more *x*'s with colored markers.
4. Press on a layer of clear contact paper to seal.
5. Encourage him to use his *x* Bookmark in his favorite books.

X Bookmark • 205

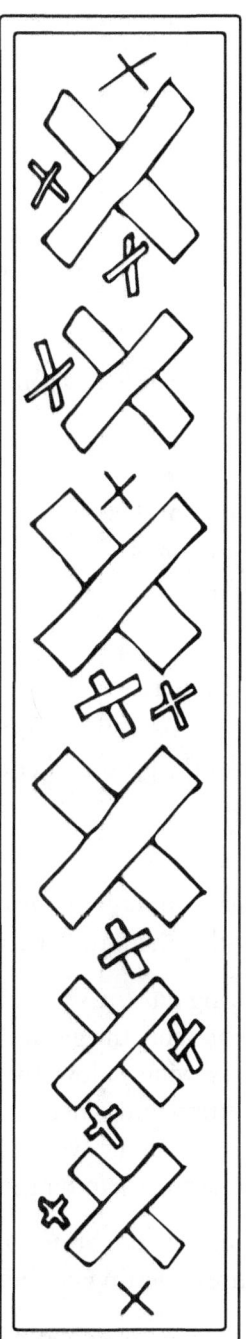

~ X ~

X Sews a Button

If you look carefully, you can find x shapes in many places. Here they form the centers of flowers.

☞ **What You Need:**
Paper, pencil, large four-hole buttons, light blue and brown felt, scissors, blunt craft needle, thin yellow and green yarn or embroidery thread

✂ **To Prepare:**
Glue a piece of brown felt onto the bottom portion of the light blue felt to make the ground. Let dry.

☆ **Activity:**
1. Ask your child to watch as you write a large *x* on paper. Have her trace it with pencil, then write more of her own while saying its sound (*ks*).

2. Bring out the sheet of light blue felt. Explain that the brown portion represents the ground. Demonstrate how to stitch a button onto the felt by sewing yellow yarn or embroidery thread through the holes in an *x* pattern and tying it off at the back. Explain that the buttons are "flowers" on the picture you are constructing. Invite her to sew on more buttons, situating them on the top third of the felt. Provide assistance, as needed.

3. Connect the button flowers by stitching on green yarn or embroidery thread, letting her help if she wishes.

4. Have her trace the *x* pattern on the button flowers with her fingers, then display the art where she can see it.

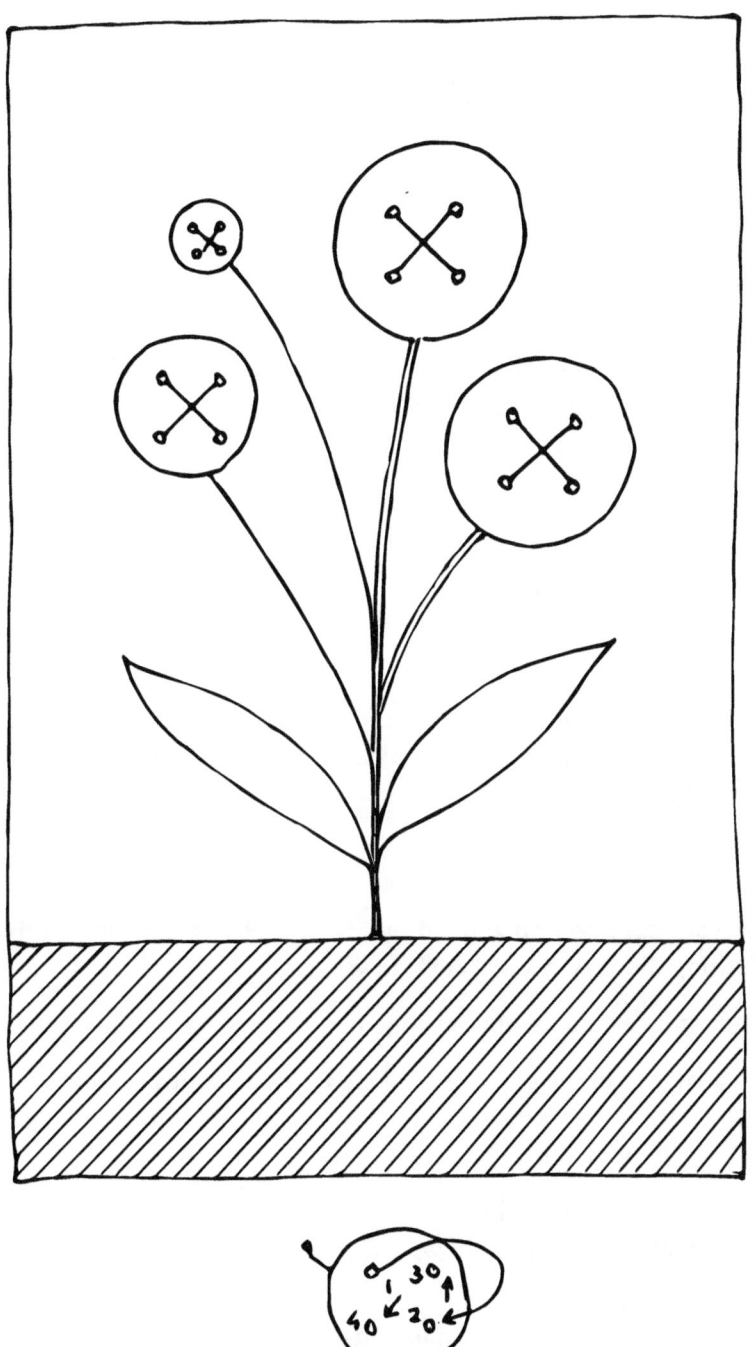

~ Y ~

Yellow Book

In addition to making this booklet, challenge your child to spy out lots of yellow things in his environment and then tag them with y sticky notes.

☞ **What You Need:**
Catalogs with pictures of yellow things, scissors, glue, construction paper or cardstock, plain paper, yellow crayons or markers, hole punch, yellow yarn

✂ **To Prepare:**
Decide on the size pages you want, then cut ten of them from white construction paper or cardstock. Punch holes down one side of each one and bind with yellow yarn.

☆ **Activity:**
1. Invite your child to find and cut out catalog pictures of yellow things such as clothing, flowers, houses, toys, towels, etc.

2. Look at and discuss the images together.

3. Write a large *y* on the cover of the prepared book with yellow crayon or marker. Have him trace over the letter with his fingers, then practice writing it on plain paper while saying its sound.

4. Invite him to glue on yellow pictures and write *y*'s on the pages. Suggest he add drawings of more yellow things such as the sun, a flower, butter, an egg yolk, mustard, etc.

5. Encourage him to "read" his Yellow Book to family and friends.

Yellow Book · 209

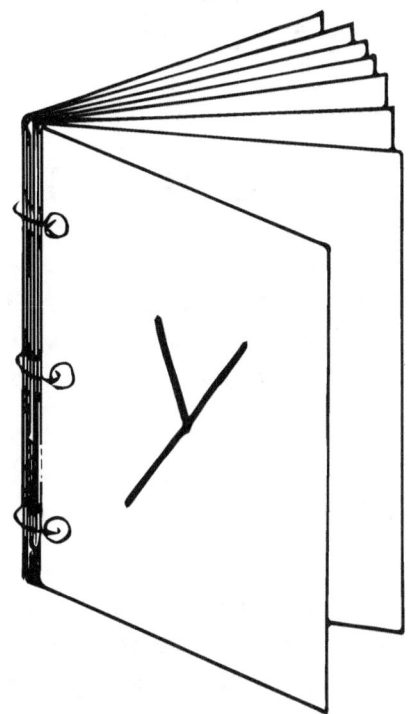

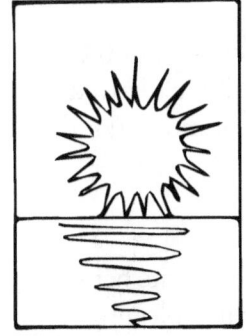 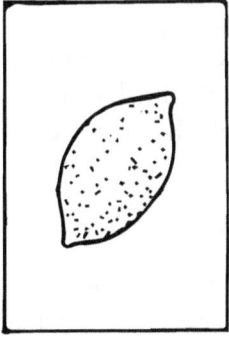 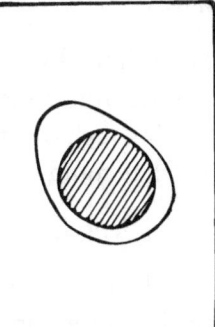 

Y

Yarn Collage

To expand your child's vocabulary, use lots of descriptive words when pointing out the yarns' color and texture. Ask questions to focus her attention, then watch her concentration and observational skills improve as she searches for answers.

☞ **What You Need:**
Different textured and colored yarns, scissors, tray, construction paper, glue

Note: Although the word *yarn* is usually used for both singular and plural, when you mean different types of yarn, the word *yarns* is correct. This is similar to the usage of *fish* vs. *fishes* and *people* vs. *peoples*.

☆ **Activity:**

1. Set out an assortment of yarns. Say, "*y* is for *yarn.*" Ask your child to say *y, yarn* several times.

2. Focusing on one at a time, discuss the texture, color, and content of the material. Does it come from a plant or animal, or is it synthetic (derived from chemicals)? Is it rough or smooth? Is it made of two or more strands twisted together? What could you make from it?

3. Have her snip varying lengths of yarn onto a tray.

4. Write the letter *y* at the top of a sheet of construction paper. Invite her to make a collage by gluing the yarn snippets onto the paper in a pleasing design. Let the project dry.

5. Display the Yarn Collage and encourage her to say *y* is for *yarn* when showing the artwork to friends.

Yarn Collage

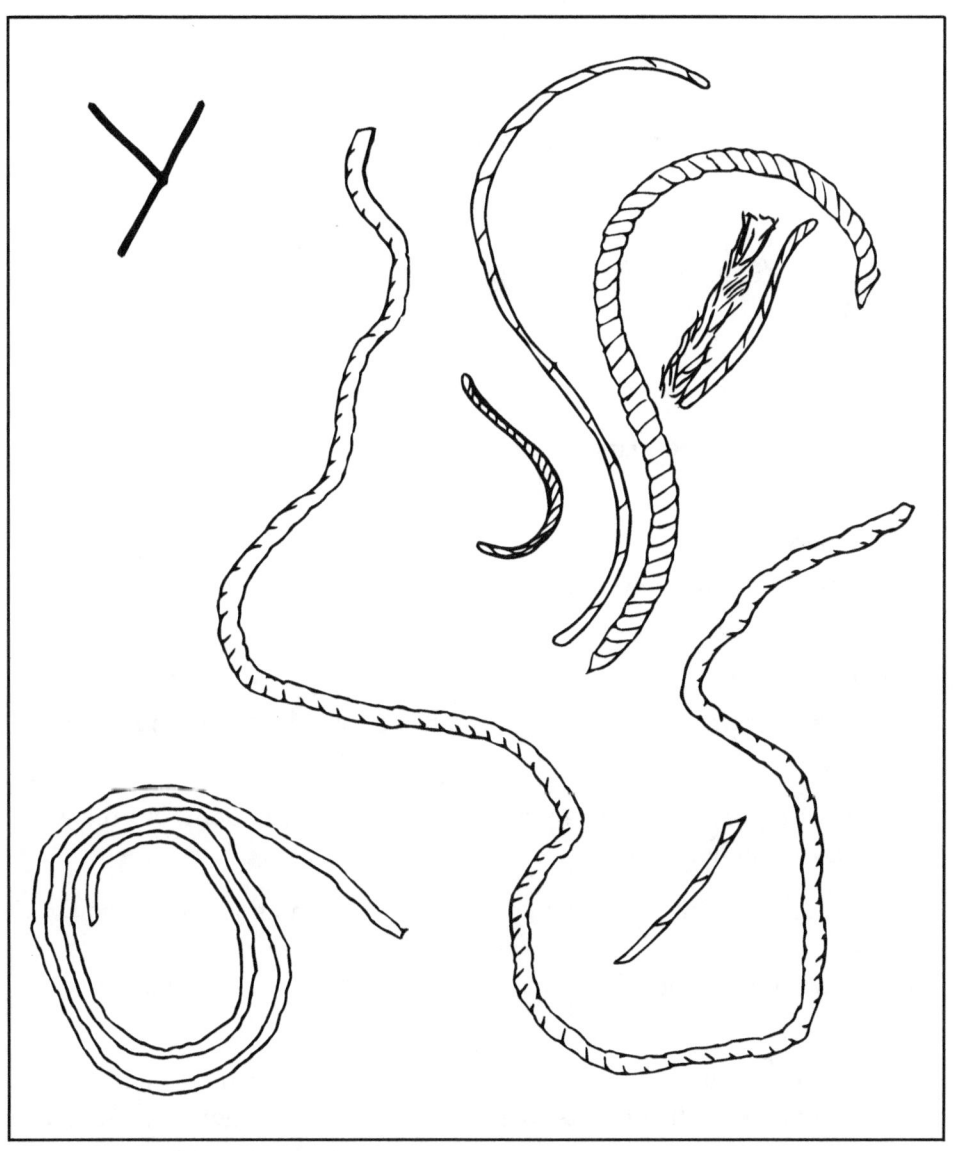

Y

Yummy Food

Use this lesson to discuss not only what is yummy but what provides good nutrition for a growing body.

☞ **What You Need:**
Paper, pencil, colored markers, scissors

✂ **To Prepare:**
Cut a bunch of one-word sized paper strips

☆ **Activity:**

1. With marker, write a large *y* on paper. Have your child trace the letter several times with pencil while saying its sound.

2. Now, write *yummy food* on a strip of paper. Ask him to point out the *y* and say its sound.

3. Explain that people have different favorite foods and that you are going to write down those he thinks are yummiest. Ask him to name some of his favorites and tell you why he likes them. Record each item on a strip of prepared paper.

4. When he has run through his list, review the items together and sort them into groups (fruit, nuts, vegetables, grains [baked goods, pasta, cereal], meat, dairy, snacks, and drinks). If he is missing some important area, challenge him to think of one or more items to fill out the category.

~ Y ~

Y IS FOR YES!

Along with highlighting the letter y, the purpose of this activity is to bring your child's attention to the many positive things she can do. Prepare many more yes *questions than* no *questions so she can give the ringing response,* Yes!

☞ What You Need:
Cardstock, paper, pencil, markers, scissors, glue, basket

✂ To Prepare:
1. Make a chart, as shown, by gluing (on three sides) two pockets to a sheet of cardstock. Write *yes* on one and *no* on the other.

2. Write questions that require yes or no answers on strips of paper and place them in a basket. Here are some ideas to get you started:

   <u>**Yes Questions**</u>
   - Can you sing a song?
   - Can you dress yourself?
   - Can you fold napkins?
   - Can you count to five (or ten)?
   - Are you happy?
   - Are you helpful?
   - Can you hop?
   - Do you brush your teeth?

- Do you have friends?
- Do you like to eat?
- Can you catch a ball?

No Questions
- Can you eat the moon?
- Can you fly an airplane?
- Do you need help talking?
- Are you as tall as a house?
- Do you live in a submarine?

☆ **Activity:**
1. Bring out paper and a pencil and have your child practice writing the letter *y*. Tell her that *y* is for *yes!*
2. Review the chart with her and set it at a distance. Ask her to hand you a slip of paper from the basket. Read her the question. When she answers it, she runs it to the chart and places it in the correct pocket, then returns to repeat the process.

❧ Z ❧

Z Sewing Card

This introduction to sewing serves a double purpose as it highlights the final letter of the alphabet.

☞ **What You Need:**
Cardstock, paper, colored pencils or markers, scissors, hole punch, yarn, blunt craft needle

✄ **To Prepare:**
1. Cut a *z* shape from cardstock and punch holes in it, as shown.
2. Cut a piece of yarn twice the length of the sewing pattern and thread it though a craft needle.

☆ **Activity:**
1. Write a large *z* on paper. Demonstrate, then have your child trace the letter and say its sound several times. Invite her to write lots of *z*'s, using different colored pencils or markers.
2. Set out the prepared cardstock *z*. Ask her to trace its shape with her fingers and say its sound.
3. Tie the yarn end to the upper left top of the *z*. Guide her to stitch the shape in the same pattern as it is written. Loop over the end of the letter and tie to secure.

Z Sewing Card • 217

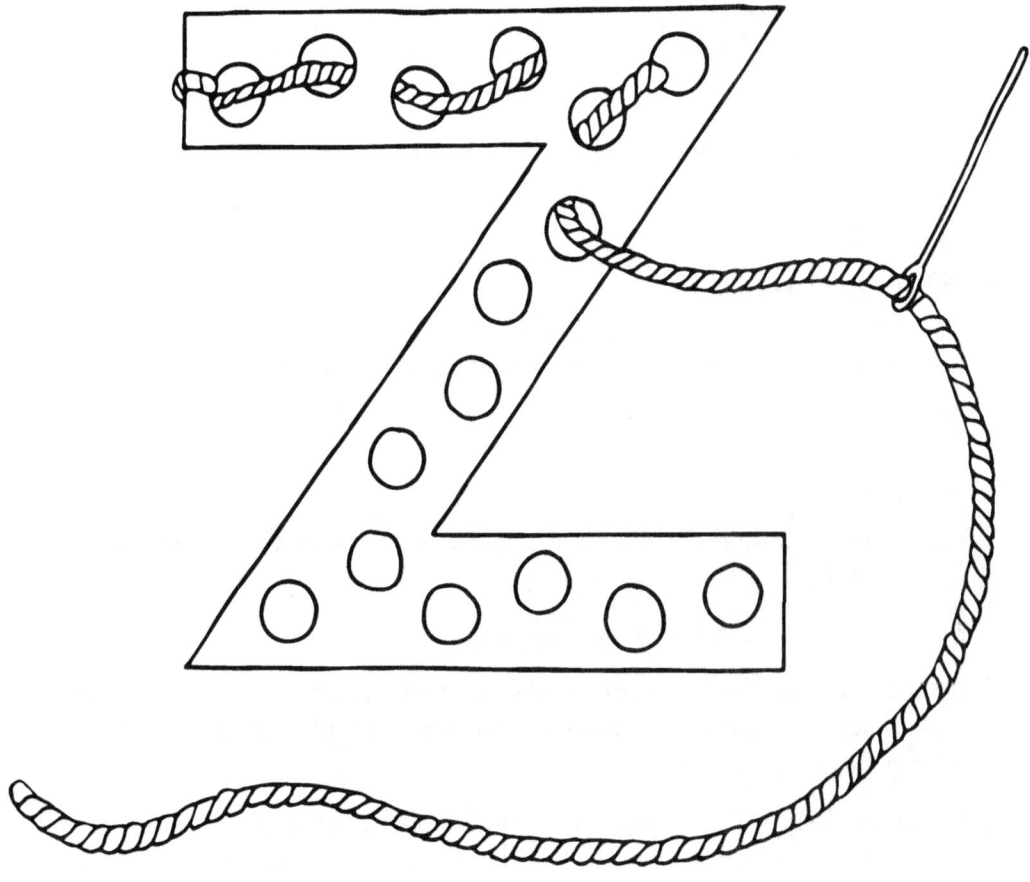

Z

Sleepy zzz Book

Just as x's can mean kisses and o's can mean hugs, so z's sometimes tell us that a person is sleeping.

☞ **What You Need:**
Construction paper, plain paper, colored pencils, scissors, glue, pictures of "sleepy things" such as sleeping animals, sunsets, beds, pillows, quilts, teddy bears, etc.

☆ **Activity:**
1. Ask your child to tell you what things make her think about bedtime and sleeping.

2. Look at and discuss the "sleepy" pictures.

3. Explain that the letter *z* is sometimes used to show that a person is sleeping. Demonstrate, then have her practice writing *z*'s on plain paper, saying the letter's sound each time.

4. Give her full-, half-, or quarter-sheets of construction paper to make the pages for a Sleepy *zzz* Book. Invite her to use colored pencils to write a *z* on the top of each page, then cut out and glue on the sleepy pictures.

5. Staple the sheets together at the side and write three large *z*'s on the cover. Encourage her to "read" you her book by describing the images.

∂ Z ∂

Z Prints

This versatile lesson works well with any letter. To get clear prints, your child must pay close attentions to his movements. Practicing activities like this improves his mental focus and fine motor control.

☞ **What You Need:**
Two new cellulose sponges, poster paint, two pie pans or styrofoam trays, large sheet(s) of paper

☆ **Activity:**

1. Explain to your child that *z* is the last letter in the alphabet. Ask him to say a few *z* words: *z, zebra; z, zero; z, zoo; z, zipper; z, zinnia* (a pretty flower).

2. Cut two *z*'s from the sponges. Demonstrate, then have him trace the shape with his fingers and say its sound a few times.

3. Pour two colors of poster paint into the two pie pans or styrofoam trays. Show him how to carefully dip a *z* shape into the paint and then press it onto the paper. Invite him to make lots of colorful *z* prints.

4. When the artwork is dry, display on the wall or use as wrapping paper.

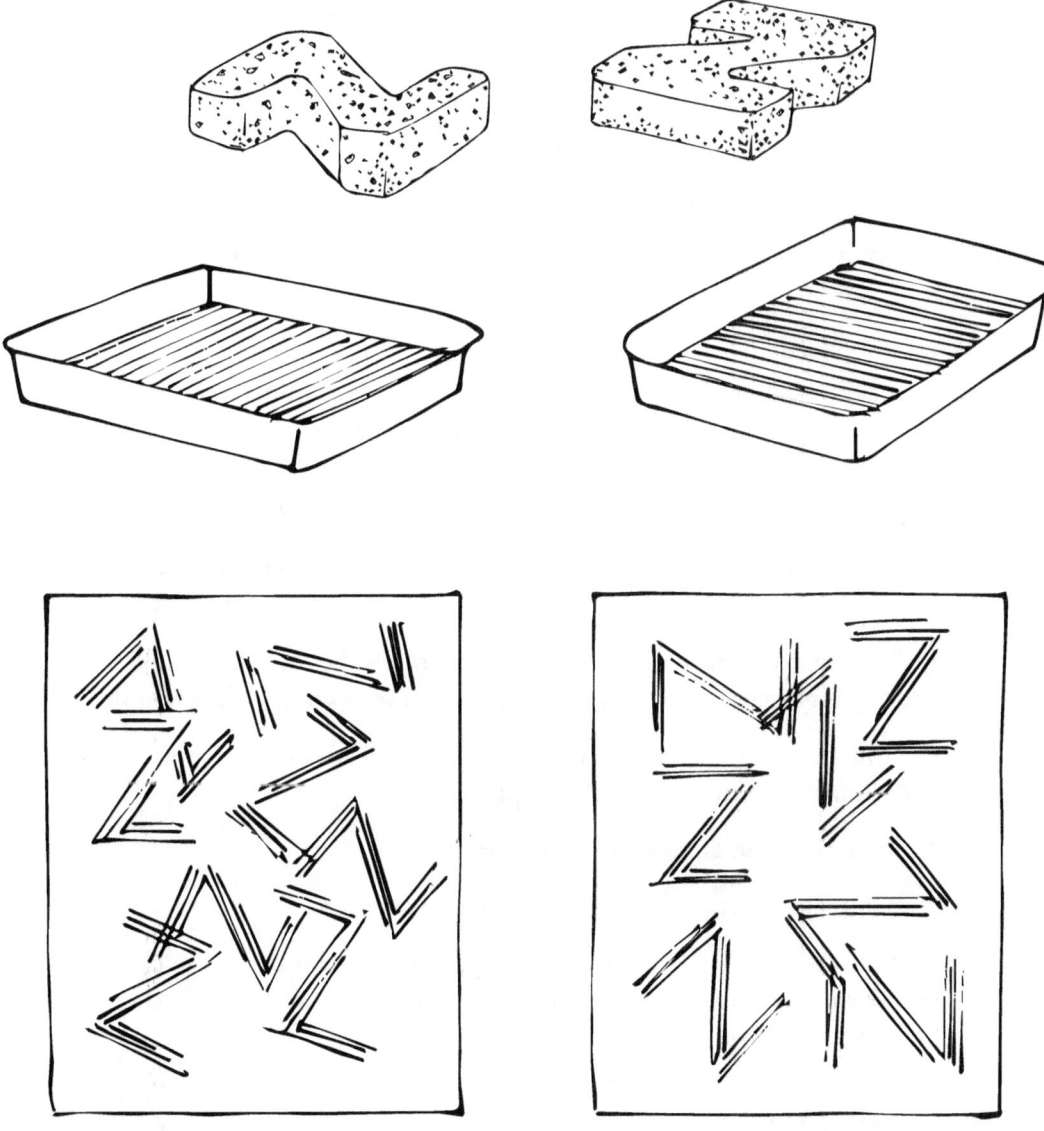

~ Z ~

Zoo Animals

Do this project over a number of days, adding new animals to the "zoo" a few at a time.

☞ **What You Need:**
Cardstock, plain paper, colored markers, scissors, glue, animal pictures or stickers, toothpicks, cardboard egg cartons cut in half lengthwise

☆ **Activity:**

1. Introduce this lesson by writing a large *z* on paper. Demonstrate, then ask your child to trace it with his fingers and say its sound several times.

2. Say, "*z* is for *zoo.*" Have him practice saying *z, zoo*. Set out the animal pictures and discuss them. Together, sort them into groups, for example:

   - carnivores (meat eaters), herbivores (plant eaters), or omnivores (animals that eat both meat and plants)

   - domestic (farm animals and pets) or wild

   - mammals, birds, reptiles, sea creatures, insects, etc.

3. Build the outline for the zoo with one layer strips of cardboard egg cartons. Discuss whether to keep all the animals in one enclosure or divide them. Does your zoo have an aquarium? If so, place pictures of fish, whales, starfish, seals, etc. in that area.

4. Show him how to make *z* flags by cutting strips of paper, folding them in half, writing *z*'s on them with colored marker, and then gluing the strips around the tops of toothpicks. Press the toothpicks into the tops of the egg carton border. Suggest he add a few more *z* flags to the zoo each day.

5. Invite him to choose an animal picture. Cut a piece of cardstock twice the height of the image and fold it in half. Have him glue on the picture or apply the sticker. Write the first letter of the animal's name on the back of the card and say it with him (*a, alligator; e, elephant; t, tiger;* or *z, zebra*).

Note: If the first letter of an animal's name has a different sound than the one already learned—as in giraffe, where the *g* says the soft *j* sound instead of its hard sound as in *get,* simply explain that sometimes the letter has another sound. Say, "the letter is *g* (as in *get*), but this time it says *j* (the soft sound of *g*) for *giraffe.*"

6. Encourage him to take you on a tour of his zoo and name the animals. Suggest he expand his zoo over the coming days.

Acknowledgments

My children were "doing school" before they realized they were engaged in any formal lessons. Smiles lit up their faces when I announced, "Let's do a project!" and they ran to their little table, eager to see what activity would be revealed. After a brief introduction, they were soon busily involved in their tasks: cutting, gluing, coloring, etc. And all the while they were learning a bit more about the project's theme. When finished, their crafts replaced older ones on the kitchen wall, to be admired—and to reinforce the lesson.

Years ago, I collected these ideas in a rough draft of this book, but lacking an illustrator, it lay abandoned in a folder, a dream unfulfilled. Revisiting the idea, I approached artist Jacob Meijer to help me. Sketching these projects was quite different from his work as a sculptor and painter, but he gamely accepted the task of bringing my lessons to life. His drawings bring a whimsical feel to the book, and I am grateful for his contribution.

Also a big thank you to Immanuela Meijer—daughter of Jacob—who patiently scanned, tweaked, and reformatted Jacob's drawings to best reflect my intent with the activities. I also appreciate her conscientious attention to detail in editing the text, which helped clarify my thoughts and eliminate confusion in the instructions.

Choosing a cover design was a challenge. I had no idea of what I wanted, just what I didn't like. Coming to my rescue, graphic designer Tara Mayberry helped me settle on a direction, and then worked with me to polish the look. I love how the vibrant cover captures the idea of letters, writing, and life!

As usual, hugs to my family, whose unwavering support sustains me as I write.

Talita Paolini

Teach with confidence and spark your child's joy of learning with these Paolini Method books!

Play & Learn with Cereal O's
Language, Math, and Science

Play & Learn with Cereal O's makes it easy to teach the basics of math, reading, writing, and scientific observation. All you need are cereal O's and a few household items. This collection of simple, effective activities makes learning fun!

- Improve coordination and develop concentration
- Learn letter sounds and discover how to read
- Write words and sentences
- Name and write the numbers
- Count and associate numbers with amounts
- Experience basic addition, subtraction, multiplication, and division
- Build, draw, and identify geometric figures
- Learn about the solar system
- Build a balance scale, measure small items, chart data, and more!

Play & Learn with Cereal O's
Talita Paolini
112 pages, softcover
ISBN: 9780966621372

Order from paolinimethod.com or any bookstore.

Read, Write, & Spell
A Complete Language Guide for Home Education Preschool–Grade 3

Read, Write, & Spell is your complete guide to teaching language skills at home. Inside you'll find a collection of hands-on activities to help children discover the joys of reading and writing, one step at a time. The lessons first establish a solid understanding of phonics and then build vocabulary skills through creative writing. Bite-sized tasks make it easy for students to complete each activity and feel a sense of victory as they progress.

- Identify the alphabet letters by sight and sound
- Read and write words, sentences, and short stories
- Create unique booklets of creative writing projects
- Develop beautiful cursive writing, expand vocabulary, and learn parts of speech
- Organize information in book reports, essays, and biographies
- Build a grammar rainbow

Read, Write, & Spell empowers you to teach your children with confidence and sets the stage for a lifelong love of learning!

Read, Write, & Spell
Talita Paolini
340 pages, softcover
ISBN: 0-9666213-4-4   Order from paolinimethod.com or any bookstore.

✦ Stay in Touch ✦

I wrote these lessons to share what I've learned as a teacher and parent, and with hope that my suggestions will make your teaching adventure easier. As you watch your child's language skills bloom, consider sharing your stories and photos on social media—using #PaoliniMethod—to inspire others with your projects.

Facebook: facebook.com/paolinimethod

Twitter: twitter.com/paolinimethod

Instagram: instagram.com/paolinimethod

Pinterest: pinterest/paolinimethod

And come visit my website, paolinimethod.com, where you'll discover more fun educational activities!